Humans in the Classroom

Exploring the lives of extraordinary teachers

Haili Hughes

Published by McNidder & Grace
21 Bridge Street
Carmarthen SA31 3JS
Wales, United Kingdom
www.mcnidderandgrace.com

Original paperback published 2021
© Haili Hughes 2021

All rights reserved. No part of this work may be reproduced or transmitted in any form or by any means, electronic or mechanical, including photocopy, recording, or any information storage or retrieval system, without permission in writing from the publisher.

Haili Hughes has asserted her right to be identified as the author of this work in accordance with the Copyright, Designs and Patents Act 1988.

Every effort has been made to obtain necessary permission with reference to copyright material. The publisher apologises if, inadvertently, any sources remain unacknowledged and will be glad to make the necessary arrangements at the earliest opportunity.

Image credits: Veronica Marx, Anchor Studio, pp.7 and 12; www.ClickClickBang.co.uk, p.34; @awenphoto Yves Appriou, p.84; Eric Rudd, p.93; Mark Blundell, p.121; Bartley Studios, p.171.

A catalogue record for this work is available from the British Library.
ISBN   9780857162229 paperback
ISBN   9780857162236 ebook

Cover design: Tabitha Palmer, Wales, United Kingdom
Designed by JS Typesetting Ltd, Wales, United Kingdom
Printed and bound by Short Run Press Ltd, Exeter, United Kingdom

Foreword

Teachers are one of the most important assets needed by society. Not only do they teach our children the knowledge and skills that they need to survive and thrive in the world, but they provide encouragement and guidance in their most formative years, when their minds need the most nurturing. None of the other professions and roles we consider so vital to the smooth and prosperous running of society could exist without this. We live in an increasingly volatile world, where the socioeconomic pressures on families are manifold; there may be days when a smile or encouraging word from a teacher may make a child's day and demonstrate that they are loved and accepted.

Covid times have shone an extremely bright light on the importance of education. Most people who work in it are motivated by the sense they are doing something important, that matters, that makes a difference. This is because we all know that ultimately education in all its forms has the power to transform lives, open gateways, change individuals, the communities they live in, society - the world. Without education we would not have any of the other things upon which our civilised lives depend. A global pandemic has shown us more clearly than ever the importance of this. This means we need to look after our teaching profession.

It is therefore surprising that teachers can sometimes seem under-appreciated, with perceptions among the public that they have too many holidays or work much shorter hours than those in other industries. Those of us who know teachers – and particularly if we work with them – are extremely aware of how hard they work and the pressure they are under on a daily basis, to do the best by the pupils in their care.

As a teacher educator, I have the privilege of working with those who are at the start of their teaching journey. It is a pleasure to see their enthusiasm and excitement at the potential they hope they will have to really make a difference – have impact and potentially transform lives. There is, however, no doubt that it is a tough job, particularly at the start of the career when it can feel like there is a need to 'hit the ground running'. This is why I am pleased to have been working with the Department for Education on the 'Initial Teacher Training Framework' which, when combined with 'The Early Career Framework,' will provide a minimum of three years' guaranteed support for millions of newly qualified teachers, ensuring that they are improving the education system for the next generation's best and brightest.

This book tells amazing stories of resilience, which will inspire both new teachers and experienced practitioners alike, but also details amazing careers teachers have had, before they entered the classroom. For those of us who have dedicated our lives to educating others, this book provides an amazing opportunity to reflect on the vital role that teachers play in shaping the world around us.

Taking on the task of shaping young minds is a huge responsibility. Teachers have the capacity to change lives, whether that is through being a role model for their students, espousing the importance of education or simply providing guidance and support. An excellent teacher is worth their weight in gold.

As with many worthwhile careers, teaching can be a complex job: there are days that are tough to get through – it really is a roller-coaster. However, there is no doubt to those who have committed their lives to the profession, that they are lucky to be employed in the greatest job in the world. This book tells the stories of just a few of the brightest and most important adults that students will come across in their lives.

Professor Sam Twiselton OBE 2021

For the amazing teachers I have known. The one who taught me and made me love German, Melanie Burras. For the ones who shaped me as a teacher: Cathy Munroe, John Sharples and Hugh Chambers. Finally, for some inspirational colleagues: Jean Hensey-Reynard and Heather Michell. If I can be even half of the teacher you all are, I will be happy.

Contents

Foreword by Sam Twiselton — iii
Introduction — 1
Haili Hughes: my story — 7

Contributors

Yvonne Conolly — 15
Kierna Corr — 20
Kyle Kiser — 24
Marco Cimino — 29
Toni Charlesworth — 34
Ash Lucas — 39
Julie Cassiano — 44
Drew Povey — 48
Bretta Townend-Jowitt — 54
Brett Bigham — 58
Jane (This teacher does not wish to be named, so we have called her Jane) — 63
Allen Tsui — 67
Michelle Alker — 73
Dan Whittaker — 79
'FreakyHoody' – Sylvain Hélaine — 84
Natalie Scott — 88
Adam Henze — 93
Jess Mahdavi-Gladwell — 98
Luke Haisell — 102
Lesley Douglas — 106

Gwen Mayor, as told by her daughter, Deborah Buchanan	112
Maureen McDevitt	115
James Atkin	121
Katharine Birbalsingh	126
Hugh Ogilvie	130
Victoria Hewett	135
Penny Rabiger	140
Joe Gibbs	146
Helena Jockel, as told by her granddaughter, Dr Yolana Wassersug	151
Caroline Riggs	156
Rachael Maddocks	161
Christine Owen	166
Sue Rogers	171
Kate McAllister	175
Vic Goddard	182
John Clifford	191
Dan Morrow	198
Caroline Spalding	202
Sarah Dearden	208
Matthew Milburn	213
Rita Pierson, as told by her daughter Kristin Wright	223
Afterword	229
References	231
Acknowledgements	232

Introduction

'Teachers change lives because of who we are as human beings: how well we listen, encourage, and help students believe in themselves.'
Robert John Meehan

It takes a special kind of person to become a teacher. This all-encompassing job will get under your skin and change you as a person ... it really is an honour and a privilege to work with young people every day.

But this book is not just about teaching: there are a plethora of instructional manuals, educational texts and journal articles you can read if that is what you are looking for. Of course, teaching is a major theme which runs throughout its pages, as it is what connects the amazing people who have told their stories. But what is most important here are the real stories behind the educators who stand at the front of our classrooms every day. I wanted to focus on the humans behind the desk and what experiences have shaped them into the educators they have become.

But what does it mean to be human? It is a question that psychologists have explored for hundreds of years. Here I am not exploring the DNA and make up of humans as a species but instead, am seeking answers about our emotional experiences and empathy ... what really makes us tick? Being human for me is more about how we see ourselves and how this concept creates a foundation for our values, morals, relationships and life choices.

In 18th-century Western Europe, the phrase "sentiment of humanity" was quite common (Mazlish, 2012). Humanity during this period was deeply connected to the notion of sympathy and benevolence and it would be fair to argue that these are two qualities an excellent teacher needs to possess today. Sometimes, our pupils and colleagues are going through emotional turmoil that we have no concept of, so we must be in tune with emotions, able to sympathise and empathise with a wide range of people. It's clear to anyone who knows a teacher that it's about much more than planning lessons and ensuring a pupil makes progress. So many colleagues recount stories of times when they have provided lunch for a student who has gone without, been a listening ear when someone in the class has been struggling with their sexuality or attended drama performances of one of their form in their own time – just to show their care. Perhaps 'benevolence' doesn't encompass the kind-hearted humanity that educators possess.

Later, in one of the first handbooks for teachers, Jersild (1955) was one of the first academics to make a link between educator's personal and professional lives. He explored the idea that in order to be an effective teacher, we must first know our own strengths and weaknesses, so that our own self-acceptance helps us become a better role model for our students. The dichotomy between professional and personal lives is something which still dominates teaching today. In my opinion, the most inspirational teachers are those who inject some of their own personality into their lessons and some of that will inevitably come from our own life experiences. We are not robots and we shouldn't be scared to show our feelings or talk about our opinions. Rogers agreed that when we allow our own human qualities to shine through, we can be seen by pupils as a "person, not a faceless embodiment of a curricular requirement, or a sterile pipe through which knowledge is passed from one generation to the next" (Rogers, 1969: 107). In short, in order to nurture human qualities in others, a teacher must show their own compassion to their class and display their own humanity to others to lead from the front.

Then, with the neo-liberal rise of accountability measures in the 1980s and early 1990s, the human aspect of teaching lost importance and was replaced with standards and reports. The freedom that teachers had to express themselves and forge relationships with their students seemed destined to be replaced by box ticking and data exercises. The postmodern era of the late 1990s brought some relief, with its focus on multiculturalism and the understanding that students' learning depended on aspects of their own culture. This meant teachers needed to get to know their students properly, in order to personalise their learning.

We have all had our own experiences of teachers; some of these will be positive and some negative. But we can all remember our favourite teacher ... if we close our eyes, their image will come to mind. If we listen hard, we can still hear their voices and recall a memory of when they helped us or went above and beyond to help us grow. What made them such an excellent teacher was no doubt their human qualities. Research has often sought to define what the human qualities are that make a great teacher. Charisma is a quality mentioned in many studies, with Conroy stating, "I did not like decorum or rectitude in a classroom; I preferred a highly oxygenated atmosphere, a climate of intemperance, rhetoric and feverish melodrama" (Conroy, 1982: 271). Perhaps the current trend of silent classrooms may find this atmosphere she speaks of uncomfortable, but she speaks of a buzz here – a perceptible zing of learning which can only be created by a charismatic, human teacher.

Another frequently cited human quality of teachers is compassion: the exhilaration of knowing that our kindness and understanding has made a difference in somebody's life. It is the "glue that binds everything that we do together in education" (Zehm and Kottler, 1993: 12). Within these pages, you will read incredible stories of compassion and kindness; the inspirational stories of humans in the classroom across the world. Their stories are unique, but it is their personal qualities that make each teacher in this book so influential. This is not something which can be imparted or learnt on a course or in a textbook. It's intrinsic. Our children are lucky to have such amazing humans in the classroom, who can help them to see their own unique talents and find their own voice, to navigate their way, so they can flourish in an ever-changing world.

Therein lies the concept of this book. All educators have laughed when pupils have expressed shock and consternation at spotting them outside of the school grounds. Even doing mundane tasks such as a supermarket shop or having your hair done can elicit an extreme reaction when students realise that their teachers don't live in the stock cupboard and do actually have a life. I find this rather sad. It is important for pupils to see us as human beings, with personalities and experiences and quirks, in order for us to be able to build a connection with them. Students often forget that we're human too. That we have problems and challenges, just like they do. That we make mistakes too. We have interesting hobbies and full lives. We do other things apart from teach and all of these things influence us as teachers.

According to recent research by Endsleigh Insurance Services (2019), 45 per cent of British adults believe that if it was not for a particular inspirational secondary school teacher, their life would not be what it is today. After all, students don't always remember what the lessons a teacher taught them were ––the memories of the way a teacher treated them and made them feel will last for much longer.

Our schools are full of passionate teachers, with amazing stories and backgrounds that have shaped and moulded them into the incredible educators they are today. This empowering collection of stories will remind teachers of why they came into the profession on those tough days and open up students' minds about what makes their teachers tick. From exciting former jobs like the rock journalist, army officer and the teacher who worked in Hollywood, to the teachers who have experienced tragic losses that spurred them on to want to change children's lives. I hope this book will be one that can be frequently re-read and dipped into, a reminder of why a good teacher is something that we never forget.

Haili Hughes: my story

My experiences would probably make me one of the least likely people to enter the teaching profession, yet now I cannot ever envisage doing anything else.

I grew up in a huge family of six siblings, on a council estate, in a Northern town, where most of my family had never studied post-16. I hated authority. So much so, that at sixteen I was asked to leave my secondary school just after Christmas in Year 11, but thankfully, was allowed to still sit my GCSE exams. Unfortunately, I didn't learn my lesson and was also thrown out of sixth-form college for not attending lessons and shirking work. Somehow, I managed to gain a place at university and completed a degree, where I finally realised that if I wanted any kind of future and escape, I had to work hard and listen to those who were in charge.

All I had ever wanted to do was be a national newspaper writer. This determination saw me giving up my holidays to work for free at my local newspaper and spending Wednesday afternoons working at a local listing magazine – again free of charge. My mum thought I was crazy and that they were abusing my good will, but I knew that to stand out from all of the middle-class kids who had gone to private schools and Oxbridge, who I would no doubt be competing against, I had to put the work in.

Despite being repeatedly told it wasn't possible by constant naysayers, I had my heart set on starting at the nationals and skipping local journalism. Therefore, I started to read the *Guardian* Media jobs page voraciously in my third year of my undergraduate studies, scanning for graduate traineeships that would give me that foot in the door. Around Christmas time, I spotted the advert for a two-year graduate traineeship at a huge tabloid Sunday newspaper. As part of the package, they would pay for my Postgraduate Diploma in Newspaper Journalism at a London university, where I already had a place. It seemed too good to be true, but I sent off my application and hoped for the best.

Weeks later, I still hadn't heard anything and was getting increasingly worried about how I could afford to pay my university fees and move to London in a few months' time. So rather bravely, I decided to telephone the newspaper and ask them whether they had shortlisted. After a nail-biting conversation with the Associate Editor, he informed me that they hadn't yet decided and would be getting in contact with successful candidates in the next week. Just a few hours later, I received a phone call that would change my life forever... I had been shortlisted, with another five applicants. They had narrowed the field down from 600 and somehow, I had made it to the next stage. Was it my pluckiness and nerve at ringing them and asking? I am sure it must have contributed in some part.

The next week, dressed in a suit, I boarded a train from Leeds to London, first-class no less (paid for by the newspaper of course) and made my way to the offices for my interview, feeling like a queen with my complimentary coffee and pretzels. Starry-eyed, I passed Tower Bridge and the Tower of London, envisioning a life akin to Carrie Bradshaw from *Sex in the City*, where I swanned around the capital, wearing designer clothes and lunching at fabulous places.

Reader, I got the job … and prepared to move to London to embark on the rest of my exciting life.

If you would have told my twenty-one-year-old self that in just five years' time, I would be studying for a PGCE, I would have laughed in your face. I am ashamed to say that my perception of teaching was like some of the general public's: working for half a day, all of those holidays, etc… I used to joke with friends that teaching was for people who didn't know what to do with their degrees and couldn't do anything better. Now I realise how rude and misinformed I was.

My first year living in the capital was a real learning curve, but I took it in my stride. I stood out on my course as the token 'working class' Northern girl, surrounded by Oxford and Cambridge graduates or those whose mummy or daddy had been journalists themselves. Despite this, the other students on my course were some of the most amazing people I have ever met. This year was one of the happiest I have ever had, as my social circle increased and I was caught up in a whirlwind of evenings out, parties and dinners at restaurants. However, having no bank of mum and dad to fall back on and a very meagre salary from the newspaper, meant that I began to fall into financial difficulties. Trying to keep up with my friends, some of whom were being bankrolled by parents, while trying to singlehandedly pay the rent on my flat and tube fares led to me living on credit cards and overdrafts. I couldn't sustain it any longer and my mental health began to decline – exacerbated by my working life after the course finished too.

Life at a national newspaper was hard. The paper I worked for was the biggest selling Sunday newspaper in the world; it wielded an awful power which could make or break careers. It was run by quite masochistic, overly macho men who looked more like Wall Street bankers than journalists, with their red ties and braces and pinstripe shirts. I remember one particular occasion I was asked to write something under quite a tight deadline and was typing as quickly as I could. Suddenly, the news editor stood next to me, screaming in my face for me to hurry up, swearing and sweating as he eyeballed me in a menacing manner. This was nothing out of the ordinary. Bullying tactics seemed to be the style of management as they knew they could get away with it. They constantly told me I was lucky. That there were hundreds of people queuing up round the block waiting for my job. They said it so often I believed it myself.

I was rapidly falling out of love with journalism, due to increasingly being asked to do things that jarred with my own ethics and were borderline illegal. It left me questioning myself as it was all I had ever wanted, and it no longer made me happy. Who was I? My family carried around my business cards in their purses and wallets, proudly telling people that their daughter was a national newspaper journalist in London. I didn't want to let them down. It seemed like the whole weight of the world was on my shoulders and coupled with my money worries and the grief I was feeling at the premature death of my beloved grandad, I broke down. On a Christmas trip to Glasgow to spend time with my dad, I laid my soul bare and he gave me some sage advice: nobody would be disappointed – if I wasn't happy, I had to leave and find something which fulfilled me more.

A few months later, I left the newspaper and moved back up North, leaving behind the friendships and connections I had made there. I watch how successful my former friends are now, filled with pride as I see them editing newspapers and magazines or appearing on

TV shows. But I don't mourn the potential of what my own glittering career could have been... I am much happier than I was then.

At home and back in my old bedroom, I was at a crossroads. What could I do with an English degree? With trepidation I applied for a PGCE and completed a voluntary placement in my old secondary school and have never looked back. Do I think my experiences have made me a better teacher? Absolutely. I know what it is to be lost, to hit rock bottom. To have the tenacity and bravery to try something new – I could help students who also felt like this.

Over the next five years my life changed at a rapid rate. I met Mike, got married and had my son Hendrix Ramone, also managing to secure a job at my dream school. Life was good and I worked with a wonderful team, under an incredible Head of English, Cathy Munroe. We were working in a deprived area of Warrington, in a difficult school where we could really make a difference. The Head, John Sharples, was incredibly inspirational and encouraged teachers to be creative and show their personalities in their lessons. By this time, I had quite a lot of tattoos and was visibly alternative. I had been into dressing in an individual way since I was a teen, but when I was a journalist, I had been encouraged to be more corporate – I had even once been sent home from the office to change as I had worn a brown suit instead of black! I loved the fact that the management at the school saw through my appearance and knew that I was an excellent teacher, regardless of my hundreds of tattoos and vintage 1940s style. I progressed quickly through the school and quickly found myself in a leadership position, loving the challenges I faced every day.

Professionally I felt fulfilled, yet personally I felt my self-esteem diminishing due to my weight. A cycle of depression and stress had left me hugely overweight and unhealthy and after an unflattering prom picture, where I looked a bit like the dad from *Family Guy*, I joined a slimming group and started to do something about it. Just ten months later, I was seven and a half stone lighter and feeling so much better about myself. Then something remarkable happened and while at a tattoo convention with friends, I was spotted by an alternative modelling agency and asked to do some photoshoots and sign up to be represented by them. I thought "Why not?" and spoke to my headteacher to gain permission. He was happy for me to do it as long as I didn't produce any images which could bring the school or my profession into disrepute.

My modelling was only ever meant to be a hobby, but it became much more than that: I ended up modelling for over 100 fashion brands and gracing the front cover of twenty-five magazines. This led to me becoming the Deputy Editor of a huge print vintage magazine and writing a column for a beautiful quarterly tattoo magazine. I had the opportunity to walk on the catwalk at London Fashion Week and compere at tattoo conventions and vintage festivals. I absolutely loved it and found myself gaining confidence every day. The kids at school thought it was pretty cool too as the

local newspaper found out about me and profiled me – it seemed tattooed, pin-up model teachers were not the norm!

Now I was fulfilled in my personal life, it was unfortunately my professional life that began to suffer, as the atmosphere at the school changed. A bad set of results meant that a visit from Ofsted loomed and the governing body needed scapegoats. Overnight, I suddenly witnessed those who were being lauded months ago being vilified, being put under pressure and forced out. I learnt a lot from this experience and vowed there and then that this was a style of leadership I would never advocate. I needed to do something drastic and step away from management. Rather bravely, I applied for a main scale teaching role sixty miles away from where I was living, stepped away from leadership and uprooted my family to swap urban living for a more rural country life, on the moors of Saddleworth. My former school has turned itself around and the incredible, hardworking staff there have achieved great things and although I still miss some of my old colleagues, I know I made the right decision.

Six years later and I love my job more than ever. I am even more tattooed and again, am trusted by leaders in the school to do my job. I feel like not being in management has made me develop my teaching skills and I am a far better teacher than I was, as I'm not forced to constantly check emails and plough through paperwork when I should be spending time with my class. I have no desire to move into a management position again, though I do now have a whole school role developing challenge across the school. This fits in perfectly with the research I am doing in my Doctorate and gives me plenty to write about in my columns for TES and the other writing I do.

Last year, after ten years of infertility and nine miscarriages, I finally gave birth to my daughter Frida Pearl and my family is now complete. It was hard to keep it together when I was going through all the losses, to be happy for pregnant colleagues and to not feel angry when I taught looked after children, who were living in children's homes when I was desperate for another child to love. But through it all, the kids I taught kept me going. My form in particular were a joy. To see them grow and develop reminded me of why I came into the job. We lost a member of our form in Year 7, so had such a strong relationship.

Like many teachers in this book, I believe that teaching is all about relationships. I live a five-minute walk away from school and I often bump into kids and parents when I am out with my family at weekends. I have to love it, as I can't escape it! I feel like all of the experiences I've had have contributed to the teacher I have become, and I often use anecdotes and examples from my life to illustrate points I am making in class. While I obviously don't divulge all aspects of my personal life, I want students to see me as an open book who they can trust. I want them to remember my humanity as well as what I taught them about poetry or Shakespeare.

Yvonne Conolly

I was the first black headteacher in Inner London, appointed in 1969, but it wasn't my intention to blaze a trail.

After I became a headteacher, in 1974, I realised that there were quite a number of black teachers in London who could have become Heads, but for some reason, they just didn't make the grade. As a consequence of this, I decided to create the Caribbean Teachers' Association, with the goal of enabling black teachers to help each other in advancing their own teaching careers in this country. I thought that if I could get a Headship, then other black teachers could too. We did workshops on things like how to write a CV and interview techniques and we met on a Saturday – it was amazing that people were giving up their own time. We held it at the West Indian Student Centre in Earl's Court, which all of the Caribbean Islands contributed to, for the use of all of their students who came to study in London. We all came together and supported one another, and it really made a difference.

After two years as Chairperson, the agenda began to change and people with more radical views began to try to usurp what we were doing. I felt that the time had come for me to leave the Association because my intention had always been to support other black teachers, but it was also about the children. At that time, there was a huge number of Caribbean children who were sent over on their own, or who were from Jamaica and had never been to school before coming to the UK. They had difficulty in using Standard English rather than Caribbean Patois or Creole. Where were the mechanisms in British schools for dealing with issues like this? They didn't exist. Of course, the school system at that time was not structured in a way to deal with this difference in the use of English.

Due to the lack of understanding about these children's backgrounds, they were labelled as "educationally subnormal." Unfortunately, this bred a sort of racism towards black children and this could be seen in the low expectations shown to these children during their school years, in comparison with their white peers. Therefore, when I became headteacher, I made it clear that I was there for all the children in my school. There would be no differences based on race or culture.

My school, Ring Cross, in Islington, had a diverse range of pupils from all sorts of backgrounds. There were West Indian children, English children, Maltese, Italians, Greek, Cypriot and Turkish children. I told the parents when I was appointed that I wanted all of these children, regardless of their background, to achieve the highest they could. We did not pressurise the children but created an atmosphere in the school which placed a high value on reading, loving stories and books. We even held workshops for parents in the evenings, showing them how they could encourage their children to want to read in the evenings and at weekends.

We also wanted to teach the children that there were a range of people in society who looked like me – a black woman. These people could be doctors, or dentists – in fact, I asked my own dentist, who was also black, to come into school with his dentist bag and his white coat and speak to the children as part of a project we were doing entitled 'people who help us.' When he arrived, the children were open-mouthed, as they didn't believe that you could have a dentist who was black! He was brilliant with them and answered all of their questions; he even obliged to lie on the floor on a blank piece of paper, so that they could draw a profile of him! We also did things where we looked at skin and hair and tried to get them to understand the concept of 'same' but 'different.' We were trying to say that they were all different, but that no one is better than the other. At Christmas time, we tried to be inclusive, singing a mixture of traditional English carols, alongside some from the Caribbean, or even some Spanish ones. There was a deliberate ethos of diversity which I encouraged in the school. Even the staff were fairly diverse: my Deputy was Australian, and we had quite a number of Hindu teachers, a Sikh teacher, an Irish teacher and so on...

Interestingly enough, it was never the children who seemed to be troubled by racial differences. I will never forget some of the nasty, racist letters I received when I was appointed. A particularly vicious one told me to "go back to where I come from," while somebody else threatened to burn the school down. I think I was probably the only headteacher who had a policeman accompany her on her first day of being appointed! A lot of the most senior people from the Inner London Education Authority also came as a kind of protection, to almost 'see me safely' into school.

Of course, in those days, times were different. Parents didn't really pick up children in cars. Instead, there were lots of parents waiting at the school gates with rollers still in their hair, wearing fluffy slippers. I could always sense if parents were complaining about something. I remember in the early days, going out and asking them: "Ladies, is something wrong?" One of them told me, "Mrs Conolly, I have to tell you, they are saying you are black!" I replied, "Don't worry about it, I am black, and I am also your children's headteacher, so don't forget it!"

Interestingly, these were some of the parents I worked with the most – inviting them into school to run workshops which empowered them to encourage their own children and take an interest in their education.

But my school was also a school of fun! At the end of the term, we used to have a party where we would invite all of the parents and community workers. We were a great community. I was astounded to recently meet our old lollipop lady, who is still working! I met her at the funeral of the daughter of my first Parent-Governor and she had travelled all the way to Oxford, as she remembered her mother from her days at the school and wanted to pay her respects. Getting involved in the community was very important to me. This enabled me to support the community committee in their battles with the Council to provide resources for children's play areas, such as an adventure playground.

I am so proud of some of the achievements of the students who were in my care. Recently, I was in Waitrose and I noticed a woman staring at me in the adjacent checkout queue. I began to feel quite uncomfortable when she said, "Excuse me, are you Mrs Conolly?" I told her I was, and she told me, "I went to your school!" I didn't remember her, but she told me that she was now a Head of Business Studies in a school and that it was because of me that she became a teacher.

I like to think that I looked across cultures and across race. I dealt with racism whenever it arose. But the main thrust of my headship was about enabling children, regardless of their circumstance, their race, colour or culture to hit the ceiling in terms of achievement.

Of course, none of this was deliberate or planned. But if, because of what I did, another person of colour can say "I can do it as well", that's great. It was all accidental, but I loved my days as a teacher – they were the best days of my life.

Kierna Corr

At the time of writing I am a forty-nine-year-old nursery class teacher in an integrated primary school in a small, semi-rural town forty-five miles west of Belfast. I am married to Oliver, who works in a local community theatre. We met at university in Derry and have been together since 1990 and married since 1995. I worked in the Student's Union for two years before being a proofreader and then temping as a nursery assistant, before then returning to do my PGCE before becoming a teacher.

I grew up just outside Belfast and was educated through the Catholic school system, so university was my first opportunity to really mix with people from other backgrounds. I studied Irish history and politics at university and as I studied in Derry, this was an opportunity to actually live in an area where a lot of historical events had occurred. I had people in my classes who had been involved directly in many historical events, such as Bloody Sunday and the Civil Rights movement. There were also many ex-prisoners studying at Magee in Derry.

I was always expected to become a teacher! My mum was a teacher; a nursery principal, and people kept saying when I was doing A-levels, "Oh you are so like your mum, you'll probably be a teacher too." But for a decade, I rebelled.

During a time when I was unemployed, I was offered the chance to fill in as a nursery assistant. This is when I finally got it – this was why my mum loved her job so much. I loved the enthusiasm of the young children and their awe and wonder at everything, even the mundane. I began to apply to do my PGCE and finally qualified in 2000. I wanted to teach nursery and was fortunate to start subbing in my current school in November 2001.

During my earlier rebellious years I had many jobs, from working in the student union and in a printers to a job in a local supermarket. These positions taught me to value a job where you don't have to work weekends and evenings and would be able to earn a steady income. I worked abroad for a few summers during my student days and I was lucky to work with some amazing people – some of whom had fled unjust regimes in China or Southern America. They had high levels of education but just weren't fluent in the English language. While working in a fast food outlet I made friends with some of the cleaners from the Ukraine and Colombia and was surprised to learn they had held professional jobs such as doctors and pilots in their own countries. I no longer see these people as migrants, but as individuals who have been unfortunate to find themselves in these situations.

I teach in an integrated school. These schools are in the minority in Northern Ireland, in that they educate children from the two main communities together. Mostly, our school system is still segregated by religion. The staff and board of governors are also drawn from the two main communities, which has afforded me the chance to actually mix on a daily basis with people from a different background to my own; it has allowed me to stop seeing people as Catholic/Nationalist or Protestant/Unionist but just as people.

Due to being educated through the Catholic school system, I have always been wary of people from other backgrounds. Before working in the integrated sector, I would have believed I had little in common with anyone who didn't come from the same background as me. Being educated separately, playing different sports and attending different churches, it felt like we had nothing 'shared' to talk about. I don't believe I was ever told anything specifically negative about Protestants but sometimes, my Protestant neighbours asked very strange questions, which showed that they had been told very bizarre things about us. For example, I was once asked why we drank blood every week and, as a seven year old, I couldn't even comprehend what they meant!

I grew up during the Troubles and attended a primary school where there were children who lost parents to the violence. We had regular bomb scares, but my own life was not directly affected beyond not being able to visit my grandparents (who lived in West Belfast) during particularly turbulent events.

Being searched when we went shopping in Belfast just seemed normal to us and I do remember my confusion the first time I was in Wales and was able to just walk into a department store without being searched. I always remember being a little scared when our car was stopped to be searched when going to pick relatives up at the airport. It was very obvious that once those who were stopping the car realised that we were Catholics, the atmosphere changed. We learned to keep our heads down, and we didn't ever dare to wear Gaelic football shirts in public – they were always worn under a more neutral item of clothing.

However, as a teacher of very young children, I do now wonder how teachers managed to keep on doing their jobs whilst there was so much uncertainty and violence going on around the young children in their classes. How they remained so calm whilst taking young children out during bomb scares is beyond my comprehension. Schools were like small communities then, and when pupils were directly affected, such as having a parent killed, the staff all came together to support the child and family.

I was lucky. I had very positive and happy experiences of school and this has helped me to ensure I provide the same for the young children in my care, now I am a teacher.

I like to think I am a positive and caring educator. I treat all children and families equally and believe that as a nursery teacher, I am sometimes the first positive experience of schooling for many students and parents. I am constantly researching the diverse ways that young children learn, and I enjoy engaging with other enthusiastic educators on social media. I am involved in many European projects which have allowed me to travel to schools across Europe, to broaden my experiences and bring some aspects of what I observe back to my own classroom.

I don't follow any ideology in particular but prefer to take aspects from many and apply them to my own classroom and approach. I am fully committed to teaching through play and hands-on learning experiences and allowing young children lots of opportunities to be active and outside.

Kyle Kiser

My name is Kyle Kiser, and I'm from a small town called Shelby in North Carolina, USA. I'm currently a Deaf/Hard-of-Hearing American Sign Language (ASL) Instructor at Blue Ridge Community College. I hold a Master of Science Degree in Deaf Studies and Deaf Education, and a Bachelor of Arts degree in American Sign Language. I have a passion for teaching ASL, Deaf History, and ASL Linguistics and I've been teaching for thirteen years in both high schools and also to postgraduate students.

Growing up as a Deaf/Hard-of-Hearing person in a classroom was a challenging experience for me. I struggled a lot in school since I wasn't always provided equal communication access. I had a craving to learn but wasn't always understood by my teachers or fellow classmates. However, I had parents who advocated for my education, to ensure I got the tools and resources I needed; if it wasn't for my parents, I would've been ignored and put on the 'back burner' like some of our Deaf/Hard-of-Hearing students are today. This is one reason why I am an advocate for our Deaf and Hard-of-Hearing community and children now – to ensure equal communication access is provided at all times when they're attending school, events, job interviews, medical visits, church, etc. I work as a full-time teacher, but I also own a very successful interpreting agency that serves North/South Carolina, that facilitates this.

I was born into a family of educators. My mother and sister are educators, and, in a sense, I feel like I was a teacher my whole life because growing up, I was always educating people about sign language and who I was as a Deaf/HOH person. When my parents found out about my hearing loss, they acted quickly and privately hired a sign language teacher to come to our home and teach my entire family sign language. Since then, I was teaching the people who went to my church, my friends, high school football teammates, my teachers who requested to learn ASL, and anyone who wanted to communicate with me successfully.

Another reason why I became a teacher was because I had a drama teacher in high school, Mrs Rebecca Reger, who was one of the most loving, funniest, and understanding teachers I've ever had. I learned about theatre but also watched how she would work with each individual student to meet their learning needs. I was visual, of course! I remembered her telling us about how much she appreciated us learning theatre, how much she loved us and letting us know her door was always open if we needed to vent to someone. Sometimes she would call the student's house to see if they were okay, or drive to a student's house if they were causing troubles in her classroom, to meet with their parents. She's definitely a large part of why I'm a teacher today. I saw how she cared about the student's success and goals. She would do whatever she could to do to help them with their accomplishments. Now, sometimes, I'll show up to my high school student's homes unexpectedly, bearing a dessert, to meet with their parents if they're being distributive in my classroom. Or I check up on them via email or through a phone call, to see if they're okay, if they've had an unexpected absence. I've learned from teaching high school students for thirteen years that by doing simple things like this, it can give students greater respect for teachers. It's simply because it shows them you care.

Before I was a teacher, I worked in the customer service industry. We owned a family seafood restaurant business that was open for over fifty years, until we closed it down in 2009. As a child, I watched my grandparents and father operate the business as a team and they were the best people to work with, since they always showed they cared about their employees and customers. They always took care of an employee who might have fallen on hard times or needed an extra dollar to keep their power on. This taught me what excellent leadership looked like and how to support people.

Later, when attending college, I was working in a retail environment. I learned about the importance of time management, organisation skills, how to listen and interact with customers, and the best approaches when training new employees who joined our team. This helped me understand the meaning of business and teaching. It wasn't a clock-in and clock-out type of job. It was an environment where we kept it fun and fresh every day! Putting a positive note in someone's lunchbox/on the windshield of their car can really make an impact on their day. Now I am a teacher, I always do my best to write a daily positive quote on my board for my students to read. One of the reasons why I know it makes some type of impact on my students, is because sometimes, I'll get distracted and forget to write a quote... If this happens, the students will let me know; it excites me that they actually read the life quotes for reflection and possibly guidance.

I think not being able to hear as well and speaking differently compared to the norm is what bothered and changed me the most. It took me a while to overcome who I was born to be and accept who I am. This experience of being bullied or pointed at by others and made to feel that I was different, means that I always try to teach my students about acceptance. I share with them my stories about being bullied and how it still affects me today. It wasn't the words the people said to me; it was how they made me feel. I bring up the fact that we're all different, but our hearts are still the same: we may speak in different languages, we may come from different backgrounds, we may look or sound different from one another, but we still bleed red and our hearts still beat the same. I teach how to be a better human being, and how to be kind to one another. These things don't cost money – it's about having integrity for yourself and those around you. It takes years to build a good solid reputation; it takes seconds to ruin it. So, I always try to be wise with my words and spread positivity wherever I can.

Teachers who teach languages, teach in a variety of ways. The path I've chosen incorporates opportunities for students to engage in critical thinking and creativity. When students step into my classroom for the first time, we will begin with an introduction of ourselves and classroom expectations. The introduction is key for the students to learn about each other and to develop a comfortable environment inside the classroom. A comfortable environment will allow me to follow my lesson plans, goals and given assignments at a moderate pace with the students.

My belief is that the only way to be an effective teacher is to work with a diverse group of students. It places me in a creative role to use key instructional strategies with students, such as: discovery, inquiry, project-centred teaching, cooperative, social-interactive learning and integrated curriculum. In an American Sign Language classroom, students will be able to discover their own language by visual items/aids/things to increase their terminology and grammar. It is very important that my students can distinguish among hand shapes, palm orientations, locations, non-manual expressions and modifier movements for ASL acquisition to happen and ASL vocabulary to develop. Social-interactive will permit the students to interact with each other by signing; this will increase their knowledge in questions and responses. In this activity, I observe so I can record/document their communication methods and strategies. Students are given projects to discover their identity, culture, history and community. My primary goal is to guide students to respect each other's opinions, work and interpersonal activities.

My approach to managing the classroom follows much of the Ginott/Kohn Theory. A teacher should communicate with the students to discover their feelings about a situation and about that student in general. Teachers who take this step will be able to build up student's cooperation and allow them to model the behaviour that they expect to see from their students. Once this has been established, I can then empower them into leadership thinking and in turn, help them build their self-esteem. The "Sandwich Method" has also always been an effective tool for me to use with students. I will begin by saying something positive about their work, and then talk with them about the negative, ending the discussion on a positive note. This allows them to think outside of the box about how to improve.

Students in my classroom should never feel attacked or embarrassed about a situation. Being in a formal leadership role myself in the Deaf community, I want my students to be able to carry on the high expectations in deaf education I set: being respectful to others, creating a good environment and empowering others in a positive manner.

Marco Cimino

My name is Marco Cimino, and I am a grade 7 to 12 teacher from Sydney, Australia. My teaching areas are geography, history, business and commerce and religious education. 2019 marked my ninth year as a teacher and, while my career goals and passions have shifted throughout this time, the one constant that has remained is my drive to provide students with the best education possible and to provide other teachers with quality professional development.

There are so many reasons behind my decision to become a teacher. I get so much from my job: I am always learning; I am surrounded by other great professionals and no two days are ever the same.

While I was growing up, I went through a variety of job phases: doctor, lawyer, architect, town planner, astronaut, priest, teacher. I had no idea that I would eventually settle into one of those roles, but it wasn't until I was studying that I had two epiphanies that really solidified my desire to teach.

The first realisation that I was destined for teaching was while I was completing my undergraduate studies. In my Bachelor of Arts, we had a unit that basically translated into 'compulsory volunteering.' Essentially, this meant that if you didn't complete 120 hours of volunteer work, you wouldn't get your degree. So, I began volunteering as a teacher's aide at a school for students with special needs. I was stationed with the kindergarten class and tried to help them as much as possible: assisting the children with lunch, playing my guitar for them – I even dressed up as Santa for them so they could take photos. Once my obligatory 120 hours were finished, I made the decision to continue to return during my days off from university.

This experience really opened my eyes to the remarkable work that special education teachers do and really helped me to be further steered towards teaching as my calling. When I eventually left, the classroom teacher I was shadowing presented me with a poster emblazoned with the words 'Thank You Marco,' along with photos of myself and the children engaging in activities like sing-alongs and jumping in a ball pit. Years later, this poster still inspires me every day to be the best educator I can be.

The second realisation was during my first block of the practicum visits I was involved in, during my Graduate Diploma of Education. I had the privilege of sitting in with my supervising teacher during the parent-teacher interviews. Within context, this experience was even stronger for me because I was a former student of the school. About mid-way through the interviews, a man appeared with his son, who, to put it poetically, seemed straight out of Kenny Rogers' Lucille ("His big hands were calloused, he looked like a mountain.") He sat down in front of us, wiped his black, greasy hands on his mechanic's tunic and shook both of our hands. The following moment is forever seared into my memory, never to be forgotten and eternally there to inspire me to be the best educator I can be... At the moment we told him that his son was top of his class, he broke down in tears of pride and said in broken English, "I have worked two jobs for the last five years to make sure he doesn't end up like me. Breaking my back to make sure my kid can have the best life."

That is when the totality of my decision to become a teacher really hit me. This was exactly what I wanted to do with the rest of my life: dedicate it to changing the lives of others.

Once I finished my degrees, I bounced around as a RELIEF Teacher for a while, at different schools. There is a lot of competition for teachers in my subject areas and if you don't have experience, many schools are hesitant to give you a long-term contract. I started to lose hope that I would ever gain secure employment, so I took a job outside of teaching. This was soul crushing, as I was so determined to be a teacher and I felt so unfulfilled.

I picked up a job as a student rights advocate at Western Sydney University, where my role was to support students who were not having the best experience at university. I went into meetings with them and their lecturers to discuss issues they had and would advocate for their rights at a university level through policy analysis, assisting the Student Union with their advocacy work.

This experience did two things for me: it made me miss being in the classroom and it made me more skilled in how to empathise with students who needed more support. After only a few months in the role, I made the decision to return to teaching, even if it meant not having secure employment. I decided that I would stick it out and wait for the opportunity to present itself. In 2013, this opportunity came, and I finally gained full-time employment as a teacher.

But then in late 2013, after only a few months in my new job, I noticed a lump developing on my neck. After a whirlwind month of appointments and tests, the lump was confirmed as being cancer: Stage 2A Hodgkin's Lymphoma. At the start of 2014, my double life began, and I was sitting in a chemotherapy chair having drain cleaner pumped into my veins, while at work, I was teaching my first ever Higher School Certificate (HSC) class. I was finally doing what I had worked so hard to achieve and had been given a Year 12 class – a massive position of trust for a relatively inexperienced teacher. I had to weigh up what to do. Did I call it quits for the six months or more it would take for the treatment and give up everything I had worked for, or did I juggle teaching and treatment?

I came to my decision relatively quickly and without hesitation: I would have chemotherapy treatment every second Friday, take the weekend to recover and then get back to school on Monday. I didn't want my Year 12 students (or my career) to suffer because of my health. This went on for six months, and I did not let the treatment get me down; in fact, I'm pretty sure school helped to keep my mind off my illness. My students and the school were extremely supportive as well and they both looked out for me as much as they could.

After six months of chemotherapy treatment, I shifted to radiotherapy and this is where I really crashed. Whilst the chemotherapy took my hair and made me look like a member of *The Simpson's* family, complete with yellow skin, the radiotherapy took away the most important thing a teacher has: my voice. As my lump was on my neck (and there was also one inside almost the entirety of my lung), the frame of radiotherapy included my throat region. After about session five of fifteen, my throat was essentially cooked. After months of stoically handling chemotherapy, I fell at the last hurdle. I had to take two weeks off from work because there wasn't much use for a teacher who couldn't speak. I felt so guilty.

After that horrific year, by the end of 2014, I was in full remission and still enjoy that status today. This has changed the way I teach in many ways. The tattoos that adorn my torso from the radiotherapy are badges of honour for me now: they remind me that I am human and can show that side to my students and form a relationship. But ultimately, they remind me of the passion I showed for my students and the drive I have to ensure they are looked after.

As a teacher, I like to think I maintain a balance between providing knowledge and skills and being relational. These are not mutually exclusive and go hand-in-hand in my view. One of my favourite quotes is from Tennyson's *Ulysses*: "To strive, to seek, to find, and not to yield." This is how I try and frame my teaching.

Now I live my life to the full and seize every opportunity I can. I am an active contributor to professional teaching journals and also present at numerous teaching conferences. I enjoy producing my own podcast, 'Oh, the Humanities! (and Social Sciences),' which is dedicated to the teaching and learning of HASS (Humanities and Social Sciences). In 2017, I was thrilled to be recognised for my work in the use of Flipped Learning by being named in the 'Top 100 Flipped Learning Leaders' in the world by the Flipped Learning Global Initiative and also in 2017, I was listed on the *Educator Magazine* Hot List. I am proud of all of these achievements, especially being awarded an Honorary Fellowship of the Teachers' Guild of New South Wales for my services to education, in 2019. I was also included on the 'Hot List' in 2019 as well. But more important to me than any accolade is that even if I have only changed the life of one child in my career, then it would all have been worth it.

Toni Charlesworth

My desire to become a teacher really stemmed from a seed of a thought that was planted by my mum when I was just a small girl. I am someone who follows childhood dreams... I became a teacher due to a chance remark from my mum. But as a little girl, I had always wanted to be a mermaid as well.

But like every little girl, I also wanted to be a pop star. One evening, I was singing and dancing in front of the TV and my mum said to me, "You're a better dancer than you are a singer." At the time, I thought I was the best singer in the world, so I thought, "Wow! I must be an absolutely incredible dancer then! From little acorns, large oaks grow and so I pursued a career in dance, which eventually led to dance teaching. But I certainly didn't take the conventional route.

I'm an Oldham girl, so alongside attending dance classes, I ended up getting involved in cheerleading at Oldham Rugby League club. Cheerleading seemed perfect for me, as I was really into dance pieces with big choreography; I was always taking part in the talent classes at school and once choreographed a dance set to Thriller with forty dancers, boys hidden in the crowd like zombies and blood-bombs in mouths, so they looked terrifying. It was like Hollywood comes to Ashton! So, I went to the try-outs and was accepted straight away onto the squad as a 'Roughyette.'

Even though I found the dance moves a bit too troupe style for me, I stayed on and worked my way up and ended up becoming friends with the older girls in the squad, who were all dance teachers. I never enjoyed that style of dancing, so I often found myself going home and making up my own versions of the dances we did. Eventually, the chairman's daughter noticed that I was a good dancer and asked me to start helping her choreograph the dances, so I had the opportunity to put in flips and some of the moves I enjoyed doing. It was then that I realised that choreography was definitely the route I wanted to go down.

At college, I found myself on a dance course with a lot of people who were ballet trained and had been to dance lessons for years – whereas I was just doing it because I loved dance and didn't have any formal qualifications, but once again, choreography was my strong point. In my first year, I based one of my pieces on an evacuee's view of the Second World War and in my second year, I based my piece on mining, as my grandfather was a miner in Yorkshire. I was starting to show a passion for social justice and the plight of people: a thread which has followed me through my career. All of these experiences just strengthened my resolve to go away to university and study a choreography degree, with the dream being to eventually set up a dance school.

I ended up studying at Dance City in Newcastle, but the degree turned out to be quite disastrous unfortunately. Again, I found myself surrounded by ballet dancers who were quite prim and proper and bitchy. The lecturers themselves fell into two categories: Prima Ballerinas or hippy, earthy, contemporary dance tutors, who wore flowy clothes and rolled all over the floor. I found myself stuck somewhere in the middle, not quite in either crowd, surrounded by classmates from privileged backgrounds, whose parents had been professional dancers. While everybody else was out partying on a Friday evening, I was sat at home eating crisps. I had this sudden realisation … was I the best dancer in the world? Self-doubt crept in, as I noticed those around me could jump higher than me and do moves that I couldn't do. My body ached. But what I didn't realise at the time, is that those were the beginning of my Fibromyalgia symptoms.

Up until this point, my plan of one day owning a dance school had not changed, but at university we were given a project where we had to go and do some work experience in the community. After a chance encounter with somebody in Iceland, where I worked part-time, I ended up getting an opportunity to go and teach some dance workshops in a woman's refuge. At the time, I was in an abusive relationship and something in those women's stories resonated with me. I spent an amazing three months at the refuge, working on a Christmas performance with the women, so they could do a panto for their families. On opening night, the audience was packed full of the women's friends and families and I thought about their journeys and how far they had come, and I was very proud. These women had been through hell and back and it was right that they should be given this opportunity. The dreams of owning my own dance school evaporated and I knew that I wanted to be a dance teacher as a form of therapy.

But after graduation, I returned to Oldham and just couldn't find a job, so I decided to work as a cleaner while I continued with my search. I got a job cleaning at Rock Street, which is part of Oldham Mental Health Service and one day, I ended up getting locked in the cleaning cupboard, for about seven hours, by quite a volatile patient they had there. I was obviously upset and by the time somebody heard me crying and let me out, I just broke down and said: "I don't want to be a cleaner, I just want to be a dance therapist!" All of my frustrations just came pouring out on this poor unsuspecting bloke. But then the ultimate moment of serendipity arrived, as he told me that they had a dance therapist in at that very moment and that if I wanted, he would go and introduce me to her! Obviously, I jumped at the chance, but on meeting her, I was shocked to see that it was Katy Dymoke – who I had recently written an essay on at university. We struck up an instant rapport and she offered me a job at her charity, Touchdown Dance.

At first, I just did admin, but then one of the dance therapists left, so I had the opportunity to start teaching some of the community classes for people with learning difficulties and visual impairments. I loved it. At the same time as running this class, I was also working at the Brindley in Runcorn doing dance sessions for kids and at a day centre working with adults with learning disabilities. I had definitely found my calling.

I've had the opportunity to do some amazing things over the years and learn incredible skills. When I learnt some sign language it helped me to make the classes more inclusive for deaf people and open the services up to a more diverse range of people. I applied for some funding with Children in Need and to my delight, I ended up securing funding for three years, which meant that we were able to work with three schools for children who have some form of special needs, across the North West.

One of my most amazing experiences as an educator has been teaching a non-verbal person to speak. We built a relationship because I saw her. She wasn't just a silent lady in a class. She had a voice, but she wasn't being heard. Other teachers had previously just bypassed her because she couldn't answer the questions. I came up with a system where she would answer my questions by pointing at parts of her body, so I would ask her questions and wait patiently for her to respond. One week, I was really surprised, as she just walked into the class and hugged me. This was somebody who hated physical contact. She started to make noises, which eventually led to her saying my name. Then when she found out that I was pregnant, she went to a market with her mum and stopped at a stall selling baby clothes. She pointed to them, but her mum was having difficulty understanding what she wanted, then she said "Mum!" She had never said this word before, so you can imagine how her mother must have felt... It's amazing to think I had a hand in that.

Being a teacher meant I had achieved one dream, so I thought, why not follow my dream to become a mermaid too?

On my quest to be a mermaid, I did a lot of research and at the time, there weren't any other mermaids in the UK. Buying the equipment, especially the tail, is an expensive business, so I saved up and bought the best tail that money could buy – it cost more than my wedding dress! I combined my dance training and work with children to start up my own company, where I did mermaid children's parties which were of an educational nature. I learnt to free dive, so it was more authentic and asked the kids lots of questions about nature and sea life, so I was still in that teacher role even in this part of my life. They loved riding on my back in the water and asking me questions, such as "How do you have a poo?" It was magical.

For me, it's all about giving something back to society and changing people's lives for the better. Surely that's what being a teacher is about, whether I am wearing a mermaid's tail or not.

Ash Lucas

I grew up in good old Grimsby and had a pretty textbook childhood. I was pretty ambivalent about school; I didn't particularly hate it but also didn't really enjoy it ... it was just one of the things I had to get through! But I had always wanted to join the military and was torn between joining the Royal Marines, as my dad was in the Marines, or getting a trade. Mostly, I just wanted to get out of Grimsby. So, I decided to join The Royal Engineers straight from school, completed my training and went over to join my first regiment in Germany at age eighteen. To some people, this would be terrifying—moving to another country at so young an age—but all I felt was excitement, as I had never wanted to do anything else and was living my dream. My family were also really encouraging of my career, as they're very military orientated, with some members of my mum's family also being in the RAF. There were no teachers in my family – only two people in the whole family had gone to university, so it wasn't something I had ever really considered.

For three or four years, I travelled all over Europe, visiting a different city every week with all of my mates; I even managed to spend six months skiing! Then in 2008, I was deployed to Basra in Iraq, where I spent three months building and fortifying camps for the local Iraqi forces. Things in Iraq were starting to wind down there to a certain extent but the threat of attack and roadside bombs was still very real. I also spent a month living in one of Saddam Hussein's favourite hotels, but by this time there was no air con and it was absolutely disgusting. However, after that, I did manage to spend two months in Baghdad, and we had air con and a bar ... so it was much better! The Royal Engineers are quite famous for using their initiative, so we managed to break into the bar and seemed to get away with it! It was like paradise, compared to Basra anyway. We also got the chance to do all of the touristy things and go around and see all of the buildings and monuments – but ninety-nine per cent of the time we were fortifying the various forward operating bases around the city.

After this, I had a year back in the UK, where I got married and then I was sent to Afghanistan in 2011. My job was to look for roadside bombs in Helmand Province, so we used to travel to vulnerable areas, get out of the armoured vehicles and search for bombs; if we found them, we would blow them up. We'd do this in roughly the same way as they did it during the Second World War: we would use metal detectors and use our eyes and our ears and the atmospherics around us to find them by hand. I remember I was once looking for a bomb for two hours, thought I had found one and ended up finding a Capri Sun. It still makes me laugh to think that I found a Capri Sun in the middle of Helmand, thousands of miles away.

When I was in Afghanistan, we had a bit of 'down time' between operations, so I volunteered to work at a hospital. I was one of the team medics within the troop, so I was working in the emergency room, patching up people and administering first aid. In some ways, you saw sights that you would see in any Accident and Emergency department in the UK: people suffering with alcohol poisoning who had mixed drinks, or a bloke suffering from heat exhaustion. But then, the US Special Forces brought in a US Marine and he had been shot in the shin; his tibia and fibia had been completely shattered because of the way that he had hit the ground. I was holding his calf and the rest of his leg in and we were giving him a cocktail of pain relief, so he was in and out of consciousness, laughing one minute, moaning the next. We tried to cut his trousers off, so we could treat him properly, but he started to kick off, telling us that they were his lucky pants and he had got married in them! But after a stern word from the Sergeant Major, we cut them off, only to be faced with Homer Simpson pants...

While all of this was going on, there was also a young boy who was brought in at the same time. He was about four years old and had been shot in the head. He was fully conscious, but the doctors and nurses were having to restrain him in the corner, to stop him hurting himself even more. I had a son at home who was the same age as him and my wife was also pregnant. Seeing this boy in so much agony really brought home how vulnerable kids are. I'd seen terrible things before, so I thought nothing of it.

Yet, over the following weeks, I found myself really struggling to manage my emotions and especially my temper – reading things on social media and getting irrationally annoyed and upset over it. I can see now, in hindsight, that I was traumatised and definitely suffering from some kind of PTSD. I was blindsided. My paternal instinct was triggered. My whole mindset of staying in the military long term massively changed. So, I made a three-year plan.

I got promoted and returned to the UK. I'd always loved coaching and mentoring, so I moved to a role in the construction school, over in Kent and this just strengthened my resolve and made me have a bit of an epiphany: I needed to get into education. I remembered a teacher who had really inspired me in my last two years at secondary school, Andy McBurney. He used to pull me in the cupboard at school for a 'dad chat' and sorted me out with some brilliant work experience with the fire service; he just seemed to always have my back. I realised, I wanted to be that kind of person for someone else. With my experiences in the army, I thought that I could be that person – at least for one person. I didn't want to walk around being a superhero, but I wanted to say something to somebody that would resonate with them, even years after.

But there was a stumbling block: I only had qualifications which would enable me to work in colleges. I didn't want to work in colleges, I wanted to teach in primary and secondary schools – so I did an online teaching assistant course, which I didn't really learn much from and sent a letter to every single school in North East Lincs, asking for some work experience. I ended up doing about five weeks working in alternative provision as a teaching assistant and it changed my life.

Prior to this, I didn't even know what AP was. All I had heard is that it's where the naughty kids go – I didn't really understand anything about behaviour. I stumbled into it but got a massive buzz from it straight away, although it was a massive learning curve.

Working in AP isn't so different from working in the army to be honest. To get the best out of soldiers working for you, you have to know how each of them ticks and know them inside and out. You are working with such a diverse team and that's similar to teaching. I've taught kids whose parents are millionaires and kids who have grown up in foster care ... they all need such diverse approaches to reach and connect with them. The power of the language we use as educators is massive. It's quite easy to shout at people to try and get them to do what you want in the army, but in my experience you have to build a relationship with people before you get them to do anything and if you can get a kid who is struggling to follow rules and regulate their behaviour doing something, that's a massive buzz.

My experiences in the army have meant that I've seen things that people don't often see—life hanging from a thread at times—and seeing life from that extreme is really grounding. So, in mainstream schools, I sometimes see teachers getting really stuck in the minutiae of a kid huffing and puffing and it can be really frustrating – but in the grand scheme of life, that is so miniscule. The perspective we look at behaviour from is that it's all communication and although a young person huffing and puffing, as an example, can be challenging to manage and support, we must teach them better ways of managing their emotions. After all, we teach children how to read and write; the same must be said of behaviour.

For me, it's all about finding the best way of dealing with kids – everybody has a certain way they should be dealt with. It's about thinking outside of the box and finding it! Young people's lives can be so complex, and they can show some very challenging behaviour at times but once you build a relationship with them, you're in a great and trusted place to make a huge difference in their lives. I mean, if everybody went above and beyond, nobody would have to.

In my role as Behaviour Lead Practitioner and also through the consultation work I do now, I am very much an open book with the kids and staff, and I am very honest about my experiences in the army and life in general. My life hasn't all been plain sailing and I always say that they can learn from any one of my mistakes If they refer to it and learn from it, then my mistake has been worthwhile.

Julie Cassiano

I often hear stories from teachers about how they had always enjoyed school, loved learning and knew from an early age that a life in the classroom was for them. This was not me. Though I had always been ambitious, I did not pass any formal exams at school age. In fact, I was expelled from school in Year 10 for truanting! It is fair to say that I didn't discover a love for learning until my twenties, when I became a mature student at twenty-five, studying from Level Two to a Postgraduate qualification.

With my background, it was difficult to focus on school with so much conflict going on at home. I certainly had a complex upbringing. My parents loved me, but both had a dependency on alcohol. My dad also experimented with drugs and was imprisoned for a few months when I was thirteen. Unfortunately, their reliance on alcohol meant my basic needs came second. Their neglect led to me being exploited by an older male, whereby I encountered abusive behaviour which was a scary ordeal and lasted for three years. To this day, my parents do not know.

After escaping this, I suffered from PTSD, which led to suicidal thoughts, and have since learnt about the effects of trauma.

After school, I held a succession of jobs: I was a factory operative, which led to a team leader position and was later promoted to Quality Assurance Technician. I also worked as a telephonist for a courier company. All of these jobs paid the bills and I enjoyed them, but I didn't feel fulfilled.

After serving some time as a teaching assistant in a school, I realised how much I enjoyed watching children enhance their understanding of the world. I thought about children like me, who struggled with school and traditional modes of learning and wanted to create a truly inclusive classroom. I wanted to undo some of the wrongs in the world.

I completed a GTP (graduate teaching programme) course in 2010 and obtained QTS. This route was known to be as good as the mentoring you received. I was placed in a good school and my mentor was sufficient enough. Like most, I found the training tough – particularly learning how to manage pupil behaviour. The school served a highly socially deprived area where violent crime rates were high. The pupils did not appear to have a sense of remorse. I could relate to this as I saw children who did not fully understand it but felt let down by society; not children who had no manners, or children who deserved harsh consequences, but children who needed an adult to role model care and compassion, forgiveness, fresh starts, and what it feels like to have aspirations and to be taught a love for learning (to feel success). Within this employment, I met only one teacher at this school who shared my ideology but she left the academic year I gained QTS, so therefore I decided to take up my NQT year elsewhere. Same authority, same difficulties but completely different ethos. I found the right school for me.

The fact that I came into teaching later in life and had experience in other industries certainly shaped me as a person, but didn't really shape me into the teacher I became. However, being a team leader provided some leadership skills that have shaped me into the senior leader that I am now. I learnt very quickly that using emotionally intelligent leadership strategies were the only methods that worked well when managing much older males from deprivation, who were struggling to cover their bills and did not speak English. The team soon learnt that I put their interests at the heart of what we did and in doing so I got maximum output from staff. I consider this to be the same strategy I later used in the classroom and with staff.

I would describe myself as a highly reflective, ethical teacher and senior leader. I consider everything to be complex and worth exploring, and I do not believe everything is as it seems. I promote inclusion to such a high standard and consider developing pupils' *personal development* is key. All learning centres around it. My aim is to develop well rounded, respectful, creative, deep thinking, independent individuals who feel safe to express themselves. Safeguarding is also a part of my role – one I find difficult and frustrating as there are limited resources and so many doors slammed closed. I don't want students to have to go through the experiences that I did. Cases often keep me up at night.

Since becoming a teacher, I notice that my behaviour management approach is different from a large number of my colleagues, due to having a deeper understanding of childhood trauma, adolescent mental health and living in poverty. I am fair, firm and consistent, alongside ensuring every child I have taught knows how much I care about them. Fresh starts are crucial, and I despise labelling children. High expectations should be expected of all children. Like with academic study, we can have differentiated approaches but not different expectations.

There is no doubt that my difficult start has certainly developed me into the teacher and senior leader that I am. I see behaviour as a potential signal. I do not judge families and work tirelessly with external organisations to get families the support they need and deserve. This does exhaust me at times, but I am determined to make a difference.

Drew Povey

I was a challenge at school but found I could do two subjects reasonably well: PE and RE. I was also fortunate to have a couple of teachers that really believed that I could achieve.

I carried on studying both these subjects through to degree level, as I was fascinated by the thinking and perspective side of RE and also the performance and psychology side of Sports Science. During this time, I had also started coaching rugby and found that I had a gift for being able to help the players to develop and believe in themselves ... although I definitely wouldn't have articulated it like that as a sixteen-year-old!

I was very fortunate that in my late teens, I was asked to coach at elite level in rugby league, which really boosted my learning in the 'people' arena. At the close of my degree in theology, philosophy, sports science and PE (great for anyone wanting to become a rugby playing monk!) I was involved in a number of coaching environments, as well as well as having numerous part time jobs, one being a teaching assistant in a tough school in my hometown of Warrington, Cheshire.

But at the end of my studies, I wasn't in a position to afford to do a PGCE. Teaching had seemed like a good option, as I enjoyed the coaching so much. Then luckily, funding did become available, so I applied to train as a PE teacher, a little later than most other applicants – alas, all the places had been taken. I was gutted!

As I left the education building, I bumped into an RE Lecturer who asked me about what I was doing now I had graduated. Eventually, she said "why don't you train in RE, Drew?" The picture I had painted in my head of what an RE teacher looked like was not very flattering ... tambourines and joss sticks, I thought. Having not initially been attracted to the idea, I quickly reflected on this and realised that I'd actually like teaching RE and most importantly, I could develop people within this role – so I went for it!

The coaching environments I've been in have been a huge influencing factor in the makeup of the teacher I have become. Not just with learning how to change cultures and mindsets, but also with observing high performance environments, like half-time team talks etc. It has also led to me becoming fascinated with the areas of people development and leadership. Interestingly, I was also a doorman for a short time, and this gave me great skills in how to deal with people in really challenging situations.

Another personal experience which has influenced my teaching came through music. My older brother is an amazing musician and we had this idea of starting a band and doing the club circuit to earn money whilst at university. This was fantastic in teaching me valuable communication and influencing skills, as many of our 'social club' audiences we played in didn't much like the look of these two lads and just wanted to line dance! Kind of like the feeling you might get in a hostile Year 11 assembly crowd.

I also think that being a 'difficult student' who wasn't particularly tipped to succeed, gave me an understanding of Carol Dweck's and Angela Duckworth's work on mindsets and grit. I really do believe that the hare can beat the tortoise.

When I first met my wife Vicki, she taught me that whatever has happened, we should step back and deal with it. Whatever happens she will say "Well that's okay," and it made me realise that this is a powerful message, because it will be okay. We just have to press pause and reflect, as things are never as bad as we initially think they are.

Another very powerful message that has shaped my thinking in the last couple of years—taught to me by a great friend of mine—was the famous quote from Michelle Obama: "When they go low, we go high." This may sound both simple and obvious, but it's a powerful way of looking at what happens to us and what happens in the world around us. The world can often be unfair and will constantly knock us to our knees, both personally and professionally. People will act badly towards us and may treat us badly, but if we can continue to do the right things, in the right way, at the right time, then our conscience is clear, as we know that we are doing right. This is a message that I believe we need to teach more today.

During my time as a headteacher and executive headteacher, I experienced many challenges where these mantras and ideologies came into good use. The school had been left with a legacy debt, not of its own making, totalling £3.2 million. These were really hard times for the staff, students and community, but we worked together tirelessly to deal with the situation we found ourselves in. The power of teamwork, which I'd learned from sport, was crucial at this time. Along with effort and a calming rhetoric, this really helped to deal with the ambiguity that we faced.

It was around 2016 that we were approached, for the second time, to explore the possibility of being part of the *Educating* TV series.

The *Educating* series was a British documentary reality television programme on Channel 4, which first aired in 2011 and ran for seven series. It used a fly on the wall format to show the everyday lives of the staff and pupils of different secondary schools all over the UK, with each series being filmed in a different school.

As a school, we were brilliantly spearheaded by a group of exceptional governors, who had supported us in reducing the deficit to £1.3 million, but we were still struggling to keep the school progressing in the right direction. There was a strong belief that taking part in the series was a very positive way to show the nation just what an incredible job teachers do on a daily basis and particularly at Harrop Fold School. As we used to say, "Working at Harrop was exhausting; it could bring you to your knees ... but it was also the most exhilarating place to work, too!" After several months of conversation, student votes and staff votes, the governors decided to move forward with the project.

Being part of a TV series was a big call to make for us all at the school. As Warren Buffett says: "It takes twenty years to build a reputation and five minutes to ruin it," so this meant that very careful exploration was needed – this was a decision that had to be made by everyone. Harrop had been labelled the 'worst school in the country' in 2004/5 and had also dealt with the worst debt of any school in the country, so the decision could not be taken lightly. However, being part of the series and showing the nation how great these kids from Little Hulton were, along with how brilliant the staff were, was something we were all very keen to do. To shine a big spotlight on this incredible journey was important work.

The show was such a success that the next two series also ran at Harrop Fold school – the first time that it had ever done so.

However, things at the school did not end well for me and several other staff. It has been well documented in the press that administrative mistakes on our school roll were made and that leaders were held responsible for this. This was a very challenging time for the school, as it went through a big change and the stability that had been there for over ten years was no longer there. It was also very difficult from a personal leadership point of view, to deal with this level of uncertainty. In all of this struggle, I believe that leaders must take responsibility for what has happened and also look to do the very best thing for the organisation first ... and themselves second. So, with this in mind, I parted ways with the school.

Whilst this experience is still painful to reflect back on, I am immensely proud of what we achieved during the fourteen years I was privileged to serve at the school and I believe wholeheartedly, that we gave the kids a great experience. We are not always in control of what happens in our lives, but we are one hundred per cent in control of how we respond to big change and challenge – whatever form that comes in. Things will be okay, particularly if we are willing to put in the effort; we are more resilient than we realise, and we can move forward.

One of the big elements of resilience that I find important, is the learning that must take place. My three-step process for building resilience, is to learn (asking what's happened?), unlearn (be self-aware of personal potholes and pitfalls) and then finally, to relearn (do things better in the future). I loved my time at the school and miss it dearly, but I have taken this learning and fabulous set of experiences into the next phase of my life.

My passion in life is to help people develop. This is why I started coaching at an early age, why I went into education and now, why I work with leaders in all sectors to help them develop their practice. Whilst there have been some knocks along the way, and no doubt there will be more in the future, this core purpose continues to drive my working life. From coaching individuals and teams, speaking to audiences at conferences, writing books and sharing social media posts, it's all about helping people to lead better and be the very best version of themselves. I still get up early every day to read, listen, learn and develop, in the hope that I can continue to share the ideas that will help people to improve; people can always develop themselves and are rarely at the point where they are realising their full potential.

Although I may not still teach every day, I am still guided by the belief and mantra that everyone can achieve, regardless of ability and background. It's about how much effort people are willing to put in. Tough times will come and it's not what happens to you, it's how you respond that matters. The final element for me, is that we make mistakes and mistakes don't make us; failure is where we gather ourselves, learn and come back smarter and better. I passionately believe that no one has hit their ceiling of potential, and that even today, we still often put glass ceilings in place. As educators, we must help young people and adults smash through them.

Bretta Townend-Jowitt

I became a teacher after completing my degree and post-grad so you could say I never left school. My only other jobs have been during holidays and a gap year – this was mainly running a playscheme, so still working with primary-aged children.

I fell into teaching after completing my degree. The other options open to me I no longer wished to pursue after completing placements at prisons and day centres – these being a social worker or a prison governor! So fast forward over twenty-five years and I am now a primary school headteacher in a one-form entry rural school in the Cotswolds.

I started teaching in 1992 – when I did there were lots of applicants for jobs; sometimes my application forms would be one of a hundred!! Finally, I got my first job in a reception class and moved within this school to nursery teacher. Within three years, I had moved to another school as a teacher in charge of nursery, moving again to a new school and onto EYFS Lead three years later. I was moving rapidly through the system and on an upward trajectory. Three years later and I secured my first deputy headteacher post – all in eleven years of teaching. So why did it then take another thirteen years before I became a headteacher? Unfortunately, it was due to some tough experiences in my personal life.

After six years of marriage, my husband JJ and I decided we'd try for a baby – nothing unusual there you are thinking – but for us it didn't prove to be particularly easy. After a few years of trying to conceive we unfortunately had no luck. We visited doctors and consultants, where we were both questioned, poked, prodded, probed and medically investigated. "Nothing wrong" was the answer; "unexplained" they said. Psychologically, it would have been easier had there been a medical explanation, but this was not to be. So, we went through rounds and rounds of fertility treatments, which meant rounds of drugs, rounds of injections, rounds of scans, and rounds of other interventions for month after month, until we exhausted every avenue except IVF. The whole experience was stressful and exhausting – both physically and emotionally.

Of course, all of these medical interventions meant appointments, mostly during school time. Even trying to get them at the start or end of the school day was met by management with comments like: "How many more appointments will you need?" or "Can't you wait until the school holidays?" There was nothing malicious about the questions being asked, nor was there an outward refusal for the appointments to happen, but there was such lack of understanding of the process of fertility treatment, and the impact of IVF on mental health and well-being. IVF and the precursor interventions are stressful enough and through the lack of understanding and constant questioning from my school, I felt exceptionally guilty for taking time off work! Ridiculous really when I just wanted a child of my own.

I probably would have felt guilty without the comments, as a hardworking Year 6 teacher who wanted the best for her class and a Deputy Head who wanted the best for her school, but this made it even worse.

So, I battled on, putting up a wall and a front to shield myself, which probably didn't help my cause as my smiles and "Yes, I'm fine" meant everyone didn't realise the stress I was so clearly under.

When I started the early morning appointments – 8.00 a.m. every morning for four or five days – we were often the first at the hospital, stood at the door waiting for it to be unlocked, so that we could hopefully be seen first and I could get back into the car to drive to school. I usually arrived only half an hour after the pupils, but I was still met with the same responses – how many days, how often, what time will you be in? I then needed some full days off for procedures which were exceptionally stressful and painful and returned to work earlier than I probably should have.

Devastatingly, my first round of IVF was not successful. I believe my stress levels were too high. JJ and I had some hard decisions to make: try IVF again, don't try again, go back to classroom teaching rather than being a Deputy Head for less stress, change schools, give up for a while, change career? I chose to stop working, to give my own life a chance. I handed in my resignation, which was accepted without question, no discussion about the possibilities of going part-time, taking a sabbatical, etc. Of course, with hindsight and everything I know now, I should have fought for other options, but this was thirteen years ago, and times are only now just beginning to change.

I had my next round of IVF in the summer holidays of 2006 and our son was born in the May of 2007. We relocated from Yorkshire to The Cotswolds when our son was eighteen months old and as I wanted some time with him, I decided to apply for part-time positions. There were very few part-time posts to apply for – certainly no middle leader or leadership posts. So, I started again as a classroom teacher, in a part-time, temporary post – luckily, with a Head who saw my potential – and I swiftly moved back up to the Senior Leadership Team and then, upon the promotion of the deputy headteacher, to my post as Head a couple of years later. It took a total of seven years to get back to the same level I had left, before the successful IVF.

As a consequence of my experiences, as a leader I am passionate about staff health and well-being and flexible working and am also an advocate for improving this in my own school, whilst helping others nationwide strive for equality for all colleagues in education.

Undoubtedly, it has made me into a better headteacher. I have already had more than one member of staff with an ill spouse and I was flexible to their needs and accommodated them. At the time of writing, my school has two part-time assistant headteachers, job share classes, and almost all teaching assistants and office staff are part-time with flexible working hours.

I also believe I am a champion for vulnerable pupils and engage well with their parents. I am tenacious and have a relentless drive to ensure these pupils have the best education and provide the emotional support that most clearly need.

Would I change the way I did things if I were to go back? I would have fought more for fair opportunities when I was going through such a stressful time, which is why I now fight for others. We are so lucky that we now don't need to go it alone as there are so many groups who support women educators or teacher parents. I am thrilled that there is a strong help and support available now, that was clearly needed a long time ago.

Brett Bigham

When I was nine years old, my mother spent the year knitting afghans for all of the employees of our family business. On Christmas Eve, she and I drove to all of the employees' houses where they got their blanket, a big box of home baked cookies and a card with a bonus inside. One employee lived in a studio apartment by himself and as we drove away, I asked my mom why he didn't have a wife. "Some men don't want to have wives," she said. That clicked with me and I was pretty confident that I too would not have a wife. I share that because it was so cut and dry for me. I was gay. That did not mean I talked about it openly, this was still the 1970s, but I just knew.

Fast forward to my sophomore year of high school and that was the year I decided I was going to make a big statement at school. I bought a pink Izod polo shirt and wore it to my ultra-conservative high school. I thought it was the bravest thing I had ever done up to that point. And the truth is, I'm somewhat amazed by what the old me was willing to do. I was out when nobody from my high school was. Little did I know then, that years later, I would fight back against a school district over my rights as an LGBT person.

Growing up, I realised how important teachers could be. When I graduated from junior high school, I was about to move away. My English teacher was this wonderful woman named Betsy Day, who was incredibly supportive of me. I am a quick learner and have a weird semi-photographic memory; subjects like spelling were very easy for me and she recognised this and changed my assignments completely. Instead of writing the words over and over, she had me make word search puzzles out of them that the other students used. At graduation she handed me a wrapped book and told me to open it later. I didn't see her give any other gifts away and I was very curious as to why I got a gift and nobody else did. It was a well-read copy of *Auntie Mame* by Patrick Dennis, with a note saying that she hoped I enjoyed her favourite book of all time. It was a great book, with a message of acceptance that resonated with me. The fact it was by a gay author and was her favourite book was another message. Thirteen-year-old me needed to read that story. Thirteen-year-old LGBT me needed role models and *Auntie Mame* and her friends were there for me.

Due to these experiences, years later, when I became a teacher, I always felt that it was my role to show up for the underdog. I always have and it has never done me wrong to be the person extending my hand to someone in need. So when I was nominated to be the Oregon State Teacher of the Year, I knew this was an opportunity to reach out to LGBT youth in the far corners of my state, who had no role models and no examples in their lives of what gay people could accomplish. I am an openly gay teacher. I am not this way to show straight people I am gay, but to show struggling LGBT youth that they are not alone.

However, only a week before I was to be presented with the award and honoured at the White House by President Obama, I resigned from my teaching position, tearfully hugged my staff and said goodbye to my students.

Why did this happen? I was told by my supervisor that I better "shut my mouth" about being gay or someone would "shoot me in the head," and then told that I would be fired if I did not follow her directions. By being named Teacher of the Year, I was told I would be representing the school and was under orders not that I could no longer speak or write about my sexuality without their permission.

Three times my resignation was declined, and I was warned that I would be in breach of contract if I left my position and would have my teaching licence revoked. Cornered, with almost no options but to submit, I discovered another value about myself. I value my right to be a role model to LGBT youth more than my paycheck; I refused to let them make an example out of me in the way they had planned. I decided we would make an example out of my situation, but it would be an example of how one voice can sometimes be enough to take on a giant.

So that is how I found myself on the steps of the White House, being interviewed by the International White House Press Corp. When I was asked if I had anything to say to support my students, I made a choice. I stepped into the ring swinging and I fought until I took down a school district.

Ultimately, it was a simple decision. I feel that any teacher that knows the suicide rates of LGBT youth has no choice but to give these students the additional support they need to survive childhood. As a gay man, this means being a role model. But this is not bravery on my part. I don't do it because I am brave, I do it because failing to do so has consequences far deeper than just leading a closeted life. When I was fifteen years old, my best friend came out to me and my response was supportive and loving. But I didn't come out to him. That weekend my friend killed himself.

That will help you understand why it has always been important to me to be out. No LGBT kid should ever feel so alone that suicide is an option over living.

By being named Teacher of the Year, I suddenly found myself out speaking to other teachers, visiting school districts and classrooms. This award makes you a spokesman for the profession on a nationwide level. I've been interviewed by the *New York Times* and the *Chicago Tribune* and when my school district fired me (citing no reason but the need for a change) my story ran in papers and news agencies around the world.

Suddenly, I found myself in this place where I never expected to be. I was being asked to teach on a global level. To explain the importance of gay youth having role models in the media, in places where LGBT rights are still horrendous, like Nigeria and Russia.

Unfortunately, being thrown in the spotlight like this has also brought out some less positive reactions, such as threatening mail and nasty social media posts. Occasionally, I would correct the grammar and spelling and return them, but for the most part I ignored them.

Yet the positives have been so incredible. The same weekend I was removed from my classroom, a co-worker told me to Google my name and the word Nigeria. That day in the *Nigeria Times*, they were running my story – they included photographs of my husband and I saying they were our wedding photos and a picture of us riding in the Portland Rose Festival Grand Floral Parade. Nigeria is not treating their LGBT people well, but on that day, in their news, they had pictures showing a gay couple being celebrated by their city. I knew that everything that was happening would be worth it if I could keep my mind on the bigger picture.

It was in that bigger picture that I feel I made some steps for LGBT people. In the long march for civil rights for gay people, there were steps that only I could make. There were moments where all gay teachers could move forward and I was the person who got a chance to drive that forward.

This came home to me recently when the Southern Poverty Law Center, one of the leading Civil Rights Organizations here in the US, used my case in a brief to the United States Supreme Court. I fought to make an example of how LGBT people, both students and teachers, have a right to be part of society without fear of bullying or prejudice. To be the example used in my country's highest court, showing how LGBT people are discriminated against, in a case demanding change, means what I went through was a small price to pay to set a precedent like that.

I knew that no matter what happened, putting up a fight for my rights was worth it because the bigger the story got, the more people saw a teacher fighting for himself and for LGBT kids. Somewhere in there, I realized my role had also changed. I was no longer just going to show LGBT kids the life and future they could have. I was going to be the one to teach them how to fight, and if I'm any kind of role model as a teacher, I'll be the best teacher and fighter I can possibly be.

Jane
(This teacher does not wish to be named, so we have called her Jane)

When reflecting on my background, I had personal experience of family drug addiction and alcoholism and lost both my parents in my early adulthood. My mum was a single parent and a primary school teacher and she did her best to bring me up, although at times it proved difficult...

I was certainly no stranger to challenging behaviour. At age fourteen, I was chucked out of school for truancy and throwing a chair at my teacher. I was repeatedly told there was more chance of me ending up in prison than becoming a real person. Words are important – this has stayed with me my whole life. I never think I'm good enough. Imposter Syndrome is dug down inside my brain due to those comments made to me all of those years ago.

Just before my fifteenth birthday, I got a joint state funded/parent pay place and was sent to boarding school. But I just couldn't settle there and was asked to leave there too, only being allowed to return to take my GCSEs. I left there with English, Maths and Chemistry – not bad for only being at school for nine months in two years.

After leaving school, things just went from bad to worse. By the time I was twenty, I was homeless and pregnant. I slept on people's sofas until I found myself a room in a squat. There were fourteen of us living in a five bedroomed house. We ate together and supported each other. The local market gave us vegetables for dinners, then at the end of every day we would skip dive for bread and other food items. We all had our own stories. We weren't the stereo-typical dirty squatters, most were young (late teens, early twenties) and held down jobs. We were just a group of people who had fallen on difficult times. I stayed there until I had begged and borrowed enough money to put a deposit down on a room in a nice house. I had also contacted my mum who was working abroad at this time and she helped me out as well.

After some time and a reconciliation with my mum, I had a place to live and set about getting myself together. But it was only when my daughter was three that I felt ready to return to education and enrolled in college to do an access course.

I passed and completed a degree in chemistry in four years. It wasn't easy and I failed the first year, but for the first time in my educational experience, a tutor at university believed in me and persuaded the powers that be to let me re-take the first year. I passed with a 2:1 in 2002. It was then I realised the power an inspirational teacher can have.

I became a teacher because I found I was good at it by accident. I was working as a Head Chemistry Technician at an international college and ended up covering some lessons. I loved it. The students seemed to like my lessons and even though I had no training, most of them went on to study three sciences at GCSE and subsequently A-level. There was no "don't smile until Christmas," for me; getting these kids to smile before Christmas was the goal. I made that my mission. I realised I wanted to make a difference to kids in my local community, so in my late thirties, I applied for a School's Direct chemistry place at a local secondary school.

To be honest, I struggled with the university process of teacher training. I found it hard to be micromanaged. The school I was at was brilliant and after a difficult day at university, I told my mentor I was going to quit. Her exact words were, "You're the best student I've ever had – if you quit, I will hunt you down and drag you back here by your hair!" She made me laugh and I promised her I'd stick it out. She was an amazing mentor and I still give her a call for advice.

At this school I met a girl who had suffered a loss and was struggling with her life. We chatted for ages. I told her that life will move on for her and it will become bearable again When I left that school, she wrote me a letter saying that she had listened and noted what I had said. Two years down the line, she was on track for seven GCSEs; she'd sought out counselling and her life seemed a lot rosier. She still missed the person she'd lost but could now remember them with love rather than anger.

My previous work experience did help me become the teacher I am today. In fact, I strongly believe that every science teacher should be a tech first; you understand the complexities of the job more deeply and I am told by technicians that my classroom is always the tidiest after a practical!

But more importantly, my life experiences have taught me that teaching is not always about being content. It's about compassion and care; telling the kids that you care and demonstrating those feelings in your actions.

Kids tell me stuff; I get disclosures all the time. They trust me. This is why I went into teaching; this is why my students get good grades. They work because they want to, and they tell me that they enjoy my lessons. One lad in Year 8 couldn't sit still and was always in trouble. He came into lessons and couldn't concentrate. We agreed that if he did some work for the first part of the lessons, he could mend things in the lab for me for the second part. His behaviour improved in my lessons and he soldered wires back together, tested the micrometers, changed batteries and generally helped out. This improved the learning for the rest of the class as well, as the disruption was reduced.

In the same class was a boy who was almost illiterate. I drew out tables and he filled them in. He sat so close to me it was almost uncomfortable, but I came to realise he just appreciated the care I had shown him. I gave him a poster of a local football team for his wall. "Where do I put it?" he said. I replied, "On your bedroom wall." He seemed genuinely shocked, "My wall? How do I do that? I've never had anything on my wall." I gave him some Bluetac. My classroom from then on was covered in pictures he'd drawn for me of my favourite footballer; he never missed my lessons and always told me when his uniform was getting too small. I always 'found' him a blazer or a shirt from lost property.

I've given kids shoes and coats, even socks. I've fed kids and they've fed me when I've forgotten my lunch.

This is what education is about for me. Educating the kids in acts of kindness. A "good morning" and a smile goes a long way. "You ok? Is there anything I can do to help?" is the phrase I think I use the most.

I have a house, a profession, a husband and three kids now … my life could not be more different from my humble beginnings. Life experiences shape us, and my young life was tough, but I learnt resilience. I am a survivor and have gone on to shape the next generation of survivors.

Allen Tsui

I officially started working at Willow Brook Primary School Academy in East London on the day that Tim Peake began his Principia mission, at the end of 2015. Unlike Tim Peake, my mission at Willow Brook continues to this day.

Stumbling into a leading role in teaching science and technology means that I think I have a better understanding of the barriers to STEM subjects for learners. I attended a secondary school in North London during the early to mid-1980s, as computers were first being introduced to the curriculum, but before the National Curriculum was fully established. My first computer was a Commodore Vic-20 and BBC Micro Model B complete with five and a quarter inch floppy disk drives for storage or audio cassettes. My parents wanted me to study engineering at university, but I really didn't have the science capital to achieve that and consequently left school after one and a half terms of A-level maths, physics and chemistry.

A-level computing was not an option open to me at the time. A lack of A-levels meant having to go into full-time employment instead of university, so I joined the Crown Prosecution Service (CPS) in July 1986. It was while at the Crown Prosecution Service that I secured myself a place at Birkbeck College to study for a degree in economic and social policy, on a part-time, evening class basis from Autumn 1993 and graduated in 1997. While studying at Birkbeck, I worked through the civil service grades, eventually ending up in a Higher Executive Officer role at the organisation's central London headquarters.

In the aftermath of the 1997 Labour landslide into government, one of the first acts of the new administration was a major organisational reform, not only of the CPS but across all government departments. The reform resulted in a major cull of staff numbers through an 'Early Voluntary Release Scheme', which is civil service speak for severance and redundancy payoffs. Watching this happen and seeing how former colleagues responded to such an offer or opportunity, I decided to make myself a strategy, should I ever be in that position – and that strategy was to find a completely different career path.

One of the ideas I had was inspired by a memory from secondary school, inspired by the 'how I see myself in twenty years' time' writing tasks. I had shown interest in becoming a teacher, although my English teacher, who set the task for me, scoffed at the idea. She laughed and told me I had no chance as my predicted O-Level grade in English would be insufficient to become a teacher.

Anyway, it was while at the Crown Prosecution Service and reaching the civil service grade of Higher Executive Officer in 1999, that I became involved in the recruitment and professional development of colleagues. Part of this role meant that I was presenting workshops and seminar style sessions for the Civil Service College, and my senior colleagues commented on the high standards of my presentation style, even labelling me as "inspirational" and "charismatic," commenting on how I made the training "accessible" through my approachable manner. Such compliments and encouragement reinforced my goal of becoming a teacher. Of course, I was also attracted to the holiday times, as I often found myself drawing the "short-straw" at the CPS, working more holiday peak times than I can recall.

So, when the Labour administration found itself out of cash before the Spring 2010 General Election, the civil service began another round of cost-cutting by reducing the number of staff and offering me a pay-off to leave. I completed the necessary paperwork, was selected to take the offer and left the civil service at the end of March 2010 after nearly 24 years' service.

I was still undecided about whether to work in a secondary or primary school, so I volunteered on two programmes that were available at the time to spend some time in both settings. The first was one called the Student Associate Scheme, where students on programmes with the Open University would be able to undertake some volunteering roles in secondary schools, with a view to entering into teaching. I did this by working with a secondary school academy, with their computing and business studies department, as I had thought my computing experience would be ideal for specialising in teaching secondary computing.

Around the same time, I also received an offer to be a reading volunteer at a primary school near Highgate Cemetery. I enjoyed volunteering at the primary school so much, that I decided to become a primary school teacher. I spent the 2010–2011 school year working in a part-time paid role at the primary school, as its audio-visual technician and then applied for a place on the PGCE programmes at the London based universities. I needed to stay close to home because my wife and I had just had a daughter. I was delighted to secure a place at Goldsmiths College in December 2010 and qualified in July 2012. I had quite a bumpy and rocky start to my time as a teacher and only completed the NQT in March 2016. It was during my first paid position that gaps in my skills and knowledge as a teacher began to unravel; this made my next placement difficult too.

I was assigned to a Year 4 class which had a boy with very severe SEN behaviour needs. The school had a SENCO, but he struggled to provide the support I needed. One afternoon, the boy hurt a girl in the classroom at home time. The girl was so upset that she immediately told her dad who confronted me in the playground and directly threatened me in audible earshot and visible eyeline of senior colleagues. The leadership team did not offer any direct support in the aftermath of this incident, except to observe one of my lessons unannounced, and that afternoon, I had my supply contract terminated. This experience gave me such anxiety that I asked my GP to refer me to psychological therapies where I required treatment for almost a year. It was the lowest I have ever felt, so I completed my therapy and went to work as an administrator for a private nursery.

It has only been since joining a school which I feel offers me the support for my professional development that is needed, as well as providing this for all its staff, that it has been possible to ensure that a full range of my effective teaching skills has been nurtured. Becoming a parent too over this time has also significantly influenced my teaching practice.

An early career in the civil service has given me some interesting transferable skills. When I began working at the CPS, some of my first duties included inputting case records on a stand-alone IBM and compiling summary reports using a dot matrix printer, but I have always had technological expertise. I completed the British Computing Society European Computer Driving Licence in 2000 and I can touch type to around 70 wpm. This is definitely something which has helped me as a teacher. I also use the British Science Association CREST Awards scheme as both an incentive and accreditation for some of my teaching and after-school clubs. But to be honest, just as important as all of my educational accomplishments, is the fact that I am a parent of a daughter and a son who are currently of primary school age. It is when thinking of their educational futures that I firmly believe, that in the field of STEM teaching and learning we need to do enough to ensure they're equipped for our future world.

My own experiences growing up have also definitely shaped me into the educator I have become. I was the eldest child of parents who migrated to London from Hong Kong in the 1960s and was schooled as the "EAL kid" during the 1970s in London. One of my most enduring memories is arriving at what became my new primary school, having moved from Camden to Haringey and having to sit for many days in the book corner and simply read, because the teachers did not know how to engage or interact with me. At the time, EAL provision was hardly recognised or only possible at a very low level. Yet when my teachers realised that I was quite accomplished at maths, I was allowed or encouraged to be integrated into teaching and learning with the rest of my class.

As alluded to earlier, my secondary school teachers were so dismissive of my career aspirations and desire to study at university, that when I found studying for my A-levels difficult, rather than be supported to finish them, I was invited to consider leaving and moving on to full-time employment with the fistful of O-Levels that I had. I am therefore really proud of myself for having secured a place at Birkbeck College, completed a degree in economic and social policy in 1997 and studied a PGCE at

Goldsmiths. This experience highlights two values I hold dearly and impact massively on the way I teach: firstly, I foster a love of life-long learning and secondly, I strive to give others opportunities to follow their dreams and aspirations. Birkbeck College gave me a second chance. I want to be able to create that second chance opportunity or its equivalent for everybody and anybody I work with.

I am very much a team player and have a "populist" approach to the way my classroom is run. This means I am approachable and open to anyone coming in to observe or scrutinise my teaching. I do this because I think it is really important to have parental engagement to support the work of the school. As a parent myself, I have first-hand experience of how warm and welcoming or cold and defensive schools can be to parents. My personal passion is centred around finding ways of making the primary curriculum more accessible, especially for disadvantaged groups. I never want a child in my care to be sent to the book corner as they are deemed as un-teachable.

Michelle Alker

I am a the proud mum of two sons – Michael and Charlie. The boys and I live in Lancashire and I brought them up with support from my mum and dad. Playing the role of both parents has been quite challenging at times; that said, I am so proud of the young men they are becoming.

I was brought up with my older brother, Steven, by my parents, Mike and Pauline. We are an incredibly close family and my parents regularly play an active role in both mine and the boys' lives.

I completed my GCSEs and went on to complete my A-levels. I didn't really enjoy college, and after completing my first year there, I was ready to drop out. I decided I'd go and train to be a nursery nurse instead – that seemed like an easier option. I went back to my secondary school to seek the advice of a teacher who taught me so much about life and who I had so much respect for and told her my intentions. She very bluntly gave me the advice I needed and despite my reservations, I went on to complete my A-levels. These secured my entry into Edge Hill College of Higher Education where I would undertake my BA Hons in primary education.

Being a teacher is something I've always wanted to do for as long as I can remember. I can remember being in my infant classes and I had the same teacher for three years – I so wanted to be like her. That was my goal. There was never any question about whether I would take another career path.

In September 2000, I moved out of my parents' home and into my halls of residence, ready to start my degree. My family were so proud – especially my grandma, who had always wanted to be a teacher herself. Before I qualified, however, she suffered a heart attack and died and never saw me qualify as a teacher.

During my second year at university, I fell pregnant with my eldest son, Michael. I decided that the best option would be to defer my final year. This wasn't an easy decision

Life as a new mum was tough, but I loved my baby boy more than anything. His father was drinking a lot and I was left doing the majority of the work bringing up our son. He told me that if I were to go back to studying, we'd end up splitting up as he didn't want me to go back and he told me, "You'll make a crap teacher anyway!" Those words made me even more determined.

I returned to university when Michael was only nine months old, and when he was thirteen months old, I moved back in with my parents making the final leg of my degree as a single mum. The daily commute, working part-time, being a mum and funding everything that goes with it was hard work but I had the support of my parents. I left university with a third-class Honours degree, which although disappointing, I am proud of my achievement with everything else I had going on.

I was so excited to secure my first teaching job in 2004. It was a maternity cover placement in a Year 1 class, but I was thrilled to have my own class and to finally be embarking on the career I'd yearned for. As the maternity cover was drawing to an end, the Head came to me one afternoon to tell me that they were able to make me a permanent member of staff – I was delighted.

In the summer of 2007, I became pregnant with my second son, Charlie. I married his father during that summer. The marriage was very short-lived though.

On my return to work in September 2008, I was told that I wouldn't be returning to my Year 1 class, I'd be teaching Year 6 – such a huge jump for any teacher! Being a teacher in the juniors was never on my agenda; I'd always wanted to be in the infants. The change was a bit dramatic to begin with, yet I soon found my feet and loved teaching the older children.

In 2010, I took on the role of Special Educational Needs Coordinator and I remained at the same school for over ten years, during which time, I spent a year and a term teaching Year 3.

In 2014, I applied for a position as a Year 6 teacher and KS2 Lead in Diggle School and I got the job! I was over the moon. As well as being KS2 Lead, I continued my role of SENCo here too. Five years later and I am still here.

Both of my boys have had behaviour issues and have sometimes been quite challenging. One child in particular I taught in Year 3 had issues too. I'd heard stories in the staffroom about this 'naughty boy'. when he came to me in September, his behaviour was the most challenging I'd had to deal with – but not always, which is an indication that there could be an underlying issue as to why he was behaving in this way. He could be the most caring and understanding boy one day and the next he could be running around the classroom, swearing and throwing chairs... it took him a while to trust me, but he did eventually and began to slowly open up to me. This is the part of the job that I love the most.

My fifteenth year of teaching was one that changed me forever – not only as a teacher but also as a mum. My class and I had the first term together and I sent twenty-seven excited children off for the Christmas holidays. Those holidays will be one that I'll never forget.

On 28th December 2018, I received a phone call from my teaching assistant. One of the boys in my class had died suddenly in his sleep – Lachlan was ten years old. Upon hearing her words, I fell to the floor. I was completely numb – how on earth does a ten-year-old go to bed and not wake up? I contacted his mum and sent her a message. I told her how sorry I was and that if it was okay with her, I'd ring her in a few days. She messaged back immediately and told me she wanted to speak to me as soon as possible.

I phoned her – that was one of the most difficult calls I've ever had to make. I couldn't get my head round it at all. There was another week left of the Christmas holidays, which I spent in a blur of grief and anxiety about going back to a class of now twenty-six. How would the children react? What would I say to them?

The children you teach become a part of your family. One of my biggest worries was how to deal with that 'empty seat.' Sounds silly now, but I could not have an empty seat in my classroom where a little boy should be sat.

I decided to completely change the classroom around and get rid of the empty chair. It didn't make walking back into my classroom any easier and it took the support of my TA to help me back in.

January 7th. It was the day the children were due back in school. They came in, as they had so many mornings before, but this time there was silence. You never hear silence in a class of ten-year-olds. They took their places and my TA and I were faced with twenty-six pairs of eyes, waiting. Usually after a Christmas holiday, children come back into school with tales of Christmas day and the lovely things they'd received, but not this time. I knew exactly what they were waiting for... talk of Lachlan.

I trembled as I spoke to them. They began asking questions. I told them I would be as honest as I could with them and try my best to answer their questions. There were lots of tears by staff and children. Although at times I wanted to walk out of the room, the children needed me to show them strength and I did not want to let them down. That first day back, we talked all morning about Lachlan: we cried, shared memories, as well as laughed at the daft things he'd done at school.

On the day of Lachlan's funeral, the children of the school lined the street outside as the cortége passed. I stood with my class with our arms round each other. As Lachlan passed by, we clapped.

As the weeks went on, Lachlan was as much a part of our class as he was when he was here with us – we included him in what we did and talked about him every day. I recall one member of staff asking me, 'What's going to happen with the SATs?' I told that member of staff that my priority was getting these children through this most difficult time at primary school.

There were times during the remainder of the year where I would just break down or one of the children would. We all knew that it was fine to do this, and we were all there for each other. Looking back, I am not actually sure what I did to help the children through their final year at primary school. It just kind of happened. What I do know though, is that we formed an unbreakable bond.

As a teacher, you are trained for all sorts, but never this. I actually don't think that any amount of training could prepare you for such a situation. The SATs came and went and even after everything they had been through, they nailed them. That particular class will always hold a special place in my heart forever.

Dan Whittaker

I'm a primary school teacher in Birmingham. It's a job I love. I have Tourette's (non-verbal) and ADHD and this has shaped many aspects of my life both negatively and positively. I have a wonderful wife and two wonderful kids. I have a great hunger to learn and at the time of writing was in my third year of my EdD at the University of Birmingham.

I was an idiot at school. We moved around a lot with my dad's work and in Weymouth, I got asked to leave a primary school due to my bad behaviour. When I got to Maidstone, I didn't have many friends and other parents hated me taking the first 11+ exams in the late 1980s. They hated it even more when I passed and no-one else did. Alas, I would've been happier in a comprehensive school. I was the poverty case grammar schools love to cite – I look great as a number, but not a face in their glossy brochures. I hated the teachers, the posh kids who teased me for being not rich... I hated having lessons copying stuff out from boards and hated being picked up by my hair, being jabbed with scissors and being called a "prick" by angry white fellas with beards and elbow patches.

My tics got worse and worse. I started developing vocal ones, although not swearing – more clicking my tongue and noises at the back of my throat. At age thirteen, I got diagnosed with Tourette's, ADHD and OCD and they gave me tablets for my tics and behaviour, which left me sleeping on the desk. The teachers loved it – the pills are rarely given for the kid in question, they're for everyone else. More than once, teachers and pupils alike would leave me sleeping through lessons and I'd wake up in an empty classroom, then panic as I walked late into the next lesson. They didn't like to miss an opportunity to lay into me for being late either.

In my adolescent head, I thought: "I can do a better job than these so-called teachers." After all, just caring for kids would be a good start. So, I dedicated myself to becoming the kind of teacher I had needed.

My Tourette's has always been a huge sore point for me. I got ribbed a lot at school for it and as I grew up, I developed ways of making sure my tics were not seen. Mostly, this involved ticcing when others weren't looking. My wife didn't know I had Tourette's for the first year, because I was so good at hiding them.

But you can't hide tics from thirty pairs of eyes.

In my first PGCE placement, in a boy's secondary school in south Birmingham, I got eaten alive by a Year 9 and 10 class. Most of the abuse was directed towards my tics – kids would mimic me to my face. It was very unpleasant. In one of the classes, a boy on the outskirts of the abuse (he would laugh but not join in) put his hand up to ask me about my tics: "Why do you move your face so much?" My reply, "None of your business," fuelled the fire.

A very experienced teacher had walked in thirty seconds before this happened, to get something from the back of the room, and heard what had been said. After the lesson, he asked how I was. He said how he was disgusted with their questions but didn't want to intervene and disempower me further. He thought I'd disempowered myself a lot anyway by answering the way I did. He asked me why I dismissed this lad in that way.

I didn't know.

He said that I'd given them a 'freebie' of something that bothered me. He told me that if the question came up again, that I should be honest, and the kids would respond well. I did. I was teaching a lesson on genetics and we talked about Project Orange and Chernobyl. A kid asked if my face movements were related. I told him that they weren't related to the lesson, but that they were Tourette's. I said how it had affected me and that it's just who I am. A few other kids asked respectful questions and I replied. It was a respectful moment where I became human to them. In that class, I didn't have a problem with my tics anymore.

By coincidence, the same wise teacher had come in. He found me afterwards and said, "When I walked in, you could cut the atmosphere with a knife. I heard that question and the discussion afterwards. The whole atmosphere changed there and then. You had the kids rapt. You became their teacher."

I carried this into my other placements and jobs. Genuinely, my Tourette's has gone from being something I tried to hide, to something I wear with pride. I now own my Tourette's. It's horrible at times – I get incredibly sore muscles, eyes, headaches and get gawky looks in new social situations. I've been asked a number of times in pubs if I'm on cocaine, or if I've got any they can score. I've had headteachers pat me on the cheeks and say, "Calm down dear and the tics will calm too" and parents asking me if I'd like to come to their mosque so they can cure me of my Jinn. But my Tourette's also gives me so much. I'm sharp-witted and have lightning quick reactions. I learn physical stuff quickly because of my knowledge of where each part of my body is. I make excellent relationships because my brain naturally hyper-mentalises about motives and emotions.

Perhaps most importantly though, is that it makes me human to the children in my care. Because of this, kids talk to me. They open up to me. They know that not only will I listen and understand, but that I *can* listen and understand – my experience and honesty disarms many of their inner barriers.

A wonderfully warm and wise headteacher summed up the effects of my Tourette's on my practice better than anyone else. I was making a joke about myself (something I'm very happy to do, especially with people I love) saying "the kids don't need to be an idiot in my classes because I'll be an idiot for them." His reply was wonderful: "Dan, you may be an idiot, but you're their idiot. That's why they love you. And that's why we love you too."

Mostly, I aim to be different from those who I was taught by. That's my main filter for everything I do. I believe it's right to expect very high levels of effort and behaviour of all children, but it's also okay to falter every once in a while. I believe it's important that kids know you're on their side and that being fragile is not only inevitable, but forgivably wonderful. It's vital that kids know they always have a chance.

I also believe in the power of the group as a whole. A strong class climate regulates itself. When people fall out of the groups' expectation though, it's vital I make sure I mediate their return quickly. In no way do I want them feeling like an outsider and in no way does it help them or anyone else. That means talking to them with candour and expecting the same in return, acting on the results of the conversation. Mostly, I believe in trust. People want to trust others even if they can't always. I also believe that trust is contagious. That's why I try to lead the way.

'FreakyHoody' – Sylvain Hélaine

My name is Sylvain and I am a primary school teacher. I have been a teacher for over eleven years now and have taught a lot of people, as I started out as a martial arts teacher before training to be a qualified teacher.

When I was twenty-seven, I went to teach at the Dulwich College in London, which is such a beautiful school – it is one of the places they used to shoot the Harry Potter movies, so you can imagine how grand it is. It was an amazing experience and the boys who attend have to spend £20,000 a year on tuition fees, but their parents know that as soon as their boy enters the school, they can be sure he will do well in life.

I was very corporate when I first arrived in London, wearing a shirt and a tie and a suit, but within a couple of years of living there, I started to get tattoos. I feel like everybody wants to get tattooed someday, but I was inspired by living in London and seeing all of these Londoners who just don't care about other people and their opinions. You can be fat, you can be skinny, you can be gay, you can be black, you can have no hair, you can get tattoos ...nobody cared! In Paris it is very difficult for a girl to even wear a skirt because there will be comments and they will be judged; people may even try to hit on them. Whereas in London, nobody cares. It was an eye-opener and I started getting tattoos right away, within four months.

At first, nobody knew that I was getting tattooed because I wore long sleeves and trousers on a daily basis. For the first three years of being tattooed, not even my friends and family knew! It took me around three and a half years to get my first layer of tattoos and I only started to get the visible parts of my body, like my hands and neck, tattooed when I didn't have any space left. Even on Facebook and other social media channels, I didn't post any pictures; it was really a personal passion. It was only for me that I did it. It wasn't that I wanted to hide that I had them, it was just that it was my personal stuff and I didn't think it was worth sharing with anybody.

I finally showed my arms to my mother and it was really difficult for her because in France, tattoos still don't have the same image as they have in England or New Zealand for example. Throughout history, princes and princesses in England have visited their colonies and have come back with massive pieces, so people looked up to them. But in France, it is still very much old prisoners they are associated with, like Jean Valjean, in Victor Hugo's *Les Miserables*. All of the prisoners who we sent to the colonies to do backbreaking work like pulling chains and breaking rocks, came back with early tattoos, like pin-ups, etc. So, it really doesn't have the same image. Therefore, my mother was quite shocked when she first saw my arms, but once she realised it was a passion for me and I started to use it to get opportunities in films, TV and photography, she was okay. However, she was the only one to question me – everybody else seemed to understand that I was just quite artistic.

I always disliked the sun, so tended to wear long sleeves and long trousers most of the time, but there did come a time with my tattoos that they became impossible to hide. But until last year, I didn't have any trouble in school – even when my face was covered. In France, teachers are classed as 'state workers.' This means, that as soon as teachers receive their registration, they cannot fire us. This causes a lot of problems and even if somebody turns out to be problematic, they are even still difficult to get rid of. So, I never had any trouble about teaching and my tattoos until this September.

But then in September, I had a complaint from a family of a three-year-old, as I had tattooed my eyeballs black and they said that he had suddenly become scared of me. They wrote to the school inspector to tell them that I was a radicalised person and that they did not want me around children. Now for seven weeks I have been in an office waiting to see what happens. I have a meeting in the first week in November, where I will find out what happens. It is strange that I never had any issues with my face or my hands before and taught happily for four or five years with them tattooed, but the eyes have been the trigger. I do see myself as only having one tattoo though – it is just one piece which constantly evolves.

I do think it is easier for a man. Everything is more difficult for a woman. Women get comments about what they are wearing, or their hairstyle. Whereas as a man, people are sometimes scared to say something to you.

The pupils mostly think I am cool. I am already quite rare in France as I am a single, thirty-four-year-old male primary teacher, when they are usually older married ladies, with their own children. It also helps that I have been in the same area for quite a few years now and have taught many of their older siblings, so they already all know about me. Some have also seen me on TV, or doing a video clip with a famous artist, so they think that is pretty cool!

It important for kids to have alternative role models but more importantly, they need to know that you can do whatever you want with your body – as long as it doesn't take back freedom from other people. I hope it will make them understand that tolerance is very important today and we are all equal. I am not interested in becoming a role model as such; they just need to know this. I want them to be able to grow and flourish and to know that a boy can be a ballet dancer, a girl can be a lumberjack. We are in the twenty-first century and we should be tolerant – it's about time!

It took me three and a half years to complete the first layer of my tattoo and I am currently working on the second layer. This is expensive but having all of these tattoos has meant that I have had opportunities which I wouldn't have had, such as working at night clubs or conventions. I live two different lives to pay for my tattoos but one day, my skin will end up fully black because my goal is to never stop getting tattooed.

The opportunities I have had really are amazing. I have even been in a movie for the Opera de Paris, called *Le Couronnement*, retelling some famous opera stories. My part was directed by Jonathan Littell—who won the Prix Goncourt 2006—an American novelist who currently lives in Paris. I am really proud of it.

When asked about how the children I teach react, I have always said that it takes children two hours, parents two days, and grandparents two weeks to get used to it. As soon as they hear me talk and see me teach and realise that I am a proper teacher, everybody is okay. I am convinced I am one of the best teachers in the world and I would rather be judged by my work than by my appearance. *Note from editor: following the meeting in November the Inspectorate permitted Sylvain to continue teaching.*

Natalie Scott

I'm forty-one and I have just moved abroad, to Grand Cayman. I have never married and have no kids – there is just me. I have always been defined more by teaching and my professional successes than anything else in my life, other than my lovely family.

Teaching was in my blood, I think. As a five or six-year-old, I would line up my toys and call class registers – my little sister was added into my childhood 'classroom' once she was old enough to sit up and answer her name. I also loved reading, devouring books at a phenomenal rate, and was always happiest sat quietly with a book. I was quite introverted; I still am today.

I was also lucky and blessed to have some amazing teachers at both primary and secondary and my high school English, Art and Maths teachers all had huge influences on me. It was at thirteen or fourteen that I decided I would teach in a secondary school. I wanted to make others love reading and writing in the same way that my teachers inspired me. There was no plan B.

I have taught secondary English since finishing university and started in the classroom back in 2000. I have had occasional blips but no real gaps greater than a couple of months. I have been lucky enough to have a fair amount of success and have travelled a little for roles all over the UK: I started in Manchester, then Hertfordshire for the majority of my career. But my work as an advanced skills teacher and on leading on teaching and learning took me to the Isle of Wight on school improvement work, a part of my career I loved.

I have had some amazing opportunities and also look pretty great on paper. I have been lucky enough to pick up a few awards: an LCoT for contributions to education at a national level, TES Blogger a few years back, and WATC Rising star award for Education and Academia. I am also a co-founder of the WomenEd movement, and both a Fellow and former director/trustee of the Chartered College of Teaching.

Teaching is the best job for forgetting about heartbreak or loss. I have had a personal life like a roller coaster, broken hearts and a failed engagement – maybe because I prioritised my job over him. The loneliness I experienced whilst working in the Isle of Wight made me realise the power of kindness and softer skills, transforming my leadership style. I joke that my personal life is like an EastEnders storyline, but it really has been. Teaching has been my escape – my constant.

Whilst I say it has been my escape, a safe place, at times I feel that I have looked into an abyss, a dark sinister hole of education. At one point in my career, I sold my soul to a MAT; the error only took a few minutes to realise and a further six months to break me. Whilst lying on the sofa broken I was told by my former exec head, to remember that there were many people worse off than me – a conversation which then took me to the refugee camps of France, rebuilding my love and passion for education and meeting one little boy in particular who helped me remember why I loved teaching and got me back into the classrooms of the UK and I guess, ultimately, to where I am today, teaching in a Caribbean paradise.

From the first moment I stepped into the bitterly cold notorious Jungle camp, I realised that, whilst the situation was horrific, it was a testament to perseverance and humanity. The camp was a thriving grassroots city – yes, it was underpinned with desperation, but kindness and hope of a better life permeated and flooded it. I was sold – sod MATs, funding cuts, marking policies and the looming presence of Ofsted; here I could teach children who were desperate for education. I could make a difference. The Jungle took me to Dunkirk; the appalling filth still managed to shock me.

Papers like *The Daily Mail* told tales of knifings and murders in the camps, but it didn't tell that on the night of the infamous Paris terror attacks, a huge part of the camp was set alight and makeshift homes and cherished possessions were lost forever. The remnants of tear gas cylinders, a constant police presence by the entrance of the camp and occasional people with visual injuries, told me that at night the camp was a different place to the one that I spent my daylight hours in. The scraps of clothing caught on the barbed, prison grade fencing was disturbingly reminiscent of a concentration camp – those I've seen in History lessons, in old tattered images of the Holocaust. I am very well aware that this sounds like I am sensationalising it, but when I first saw those fences, a cold shiver swept through my whole body and I inwardly gasped. Another teacher who I was with felt the same. They go on for miles and miles. The children there looked just like the teenagers that I taught GCSE to in the UK, except this lost generation were not getting regular education of any sort at that time.

When I moved to the Grande-Synthe camp in Dunkirk, which is about half an hour away from the migrant camp in Calais known as The Jungle, it had a different sort of resident, and a feel of its own. Whilst Calais grew rapidly into a sprawling city, Dunkirk was in its shadow, lesser known and until recently under the radar of the media. They did not have access to the facilities, amenities or the infrastructure that those in Calais did. I was told there were somewhere in the region of 2,000 refugees here and could only count fifteen portaloos on the whole site. These were steam cleaned by the French authorities regularly, where the dirty water poured out into the sticky mud and created puddles on the main pathway that went through the camp.

The school tent was down a makeshift path made of wooden pallets, covered in chicken wire to lessen the chance of slipping (not that effective, sadly and sometimes it felt safer to go off piste and brave the mud and weeds), then over a makeshift bridge. The green grass that once covered the park was now gone and mud ruled supreme.

The children walked to school, as many do in the UK. Some children came to school with us as we walked through the camp in the morning and we stopped on the way, pointed at cats and said 'cat' together, smiling and shouting 'chicken' and 'poulet' as we were an international school and French was the local language that they needed and wanted to learn too.

I remember one day, we wanted to teach the children the alphabet. After sitting and doing some work inside, we decided to go into the playground for some more active learning. We started off in a circle and moved around holding hands and sang the alphabet, but then moved onto body parts. "Heads, shoulders, knees and toes." We moved on to "and eyes and ears and mouth and nose." The little girl next to me, wrapped up, with hands in pink gloves was very excited. She did the 'eyes' bit perfectly but got stuck on the word for ears. I pointed to my ear, pulled it out with my cold fingers and hoped she would remember the word. She didn't, but instead beamed at me, the grin spread across her flushed cheeks and she proudly screamed "EYES!" Instantly I realised my mistake. I smiled and we started again. After a few attempts she got it. Progress!

I learned so much about empathy and humanity (ironically whilst in the squalor and breathing bitter air) in the illegal refugee camps of Northern France. This vivid humanity and perseverance in the face of adversity absolutely changed me, as the manner in which these people treated one another, and me, was in direct contrast to the cruel and cold behaviours bred by leadership in the London MAT school that had left me broken.

These days I smile way more than I frown. I love the sea air and sun on my face. Life can be tough, but a glimmer of sun and a gentle word can change a person's life.

I believe that children are more than a target grade. I believe in equity, challenge, support and humour. Respect is essential, and children like rules. Emotional intelligence is also important; there is usually something going on behind a person's actions. My lessons are pacey but not gimmicky, as education is serious business. I take it seriously and would never waste my students' time. Education is everything – it changes lives.

Adam Henze

When I was in school, it was my teachers who saved my life. I have bipolar disorder and did not have the skills or coping mechanisms to lead a happy and fulfilling life. As a result of this, I struggled to make friends and participate in school. It was my humanities teachers who showed up for me: my art teachers; my theatre teachers; my journalism teachers; my speech and debate coaches. They taught me that I had a voice and how to use it, and now I lead a happy and fulfilling life.

But for the longest time, I never wanted to enter a classroom again. School was no fun for me, so I certainly didn't see the value in being an educator.

After college, I started taking my work as a poet more seriously and performing more in public, touring around the poetry slam circuit in the United States. After an event, about twelve years ago, a teacher asked me if I would come and visit her class to perform some of my poems. While spoken word in schools is fairly common today, it wasn't twelve years ago, but I thought, why not? I had the best day of my life. It was a rural school and we wrote poems about everything they loved: tractor pulls, video games, country music, wrestling. I was inspired because poetry seemed so out of reach when I was their age. I hated my poetry units! From then on, I became more open-minded to the idea of being an educator.

A few months later, another educator invited me into their classroom, and I was surprised to hear that her classroom was set in a maximum-security juvenile detention facility. We would write poems about science things and then we would write poetry where we apologised for things, or where they would like to go back to a time where they were happy. We were using poetry as a tool for directing a conversation, either to something else or toward the self, really as a kind of basic literacy process for getting kids to think about how to have a conversation. One of their biggest obstacles is going to be conversation. They're going to have to talk to a judge and have to talk to their parole officer, they'll have to talk to an employer and explain why they have this mark on their background. If they're able to articulate themselves in a poem, they can articulate themselves to anybody, is my basic premise.

It's rewarding but it's also challenging; with prison stories, there's always some sadness to it. My friend, who's a poet, went to visit the women's facility I work at around eight years ago and there are still women who carry around her book. So, for me as an educator, if someone carried around my book for eight years, that's an amazing display of commitment to literacy and learning and reading. So, you see people making great strides and those are always really powerful, but sometimes, if something good happens to one of my students, then their name comes back into the media and then there starts to be scrutiny about celebrating them, particularly if they have a victim, then often that can lead to bad things ... there's a lot of contending with shame. A lot of our conversation from an illiteracy standpoint is about what the worth of words are, because if we can choose worthwhile words, then we can think of words that are worthy of us. I very much approach literacy from that identity-based focus; that we're reclaiming our stories. We all have to atone for things. We all have to contend with things. We should all take audits of ourselves.

This work was meaningful to me because it was an opportunity to hear the stories of vulnerable learners. This experience has led to me becoming the director of a literacy and creative writing program in American prisons called "Power of a Sentence," and I have spent years working with youth and adult students in incarcerated classrooms.

My goal as an educator is to make sure that teachers in Indiana have fun and engaging lesson content for all their students. So, my friends and I had decided to start a non-profit organisation, which was dedicated to teaching writing and communication skills to people, through the vehicle of poetry. This led to me deciding to pursue a Masters degree in the art of teaching in 2010 and I am now working on a Doctorate in the field of literacy, culture and language education.

As well as now working at Indiana University, I make a living as a poet and teaching artist. I have lectured and performed in the United States, Canada, Ireland and England and this Spring, I am setting up a tour in the United Arab Emirates. This work has brought me to some remarkable places, including elementary, middle, and high schools, colleges and universities, as well as less conventional teaching settings like alternative schools, libraries, and community centres. I have taught at a military academy, at a Goodwill, and in a drug treatment centre. But I believe that poetry is a universal language that can be used as a vehicle for teaching people how to be a good communicator for any learner, in any setting.

I have experiences every day that change the way that I teach. Big changes have come especially when I have made mistakes. They say teachers make 5,000 decisions every day, so every day I have made mistakes! Sometimes, those mistakes have impacted students in ways that I did not intend, and my approach to teaching changed because I have learned to listen and adapt to the needs of my students.

My approaches have definitely changed due to my own journey. I have been in graduate school since 2010 and my access to knowledge has made me consider my own praxis and ways of conducting myself in a classroom. Along with this access to knowledge, has come an access to power and now that I have climbed the ranks in educational institutions, I am more sensitive about my role as a gatekeeper in the classroom. My praxis is constantly a conversation about how my views and ideologies are ever shifting, and how I need to change my approach as a professional communicator if I am meant to be heard in a way that others deem productive.

Teaching in prisons can be very chaotic; I've had classes where my students don't show up and then there is a miscount and they have to go to lockdown. I've had moments where I get stuck in the prison, or half of my classes pull out and I don't know where they are, so I constantly have to adjust. I constantly have to throw lesson plans out! It's really easy to talk about vulnerable populations in terms of what they don't have and the deficits, so we focus on what we have and what we bring to the table, what our experiences are and why they're valid.

But then there are just times where I assume that everyone understands the concept or understands the vocabulary or words that I am using and then, when they don't, we just have to stop everything and start over again at a fundamental level. It's because a lot of them had a really bad relationship with school and school was their first interaction with the police and getting into the criminal justice system. A lot of times, it's their first interaction with a power, or the first time someone tells them that the music they listen to isn't worthy and the things that they read aren't worthy. A lot of what we do is untangling that and that's where I feel like that's my space. I had that same relationship to school. I didn't see the value and I just feel lucky that I ended up in a different place than my students did.

Jess Mahdavi-Gladwell

I was brought up in a mining village in South Yorkshire – my dad came over from Iran to study and met my mum. As a small child, I spent lots of time with my grandparents and great grandparents and I always found learning easy and motivating. But then at A-level, things got a bit harder.

I found that I couldn't just remember everything from the lessons and had to learn to revise; I went from easily getting grade A's to really having to work at learning. It made my time in sixth form more challenging academically but this, although stressful and not fun at the time, was good preparation for university. By the time I got to degree level, I was much better at self-initiated learning and used to not relying on remembering everything I heard just once.

I went on to university to study psychology in London and ended up staying on to do my PhD, which I submitted at twenty-five. During my Post Doc, I carried out the first piece of research into cyberbullying, which I am proud to say has been cited over 1,500 times.

But my academic road to becoming a teacher has not been easy. When I was twenty-seven, I became a mum. I had always planned to be a stay-at-home parent, not least because I had no family nearby. I found it difficult to change how I self-identified (at some point I had to stop saying I was a research psychologist when I wasn't working) and I was at risk of being very bored. Luckily, attending NCT classes allowed me to meet another mum who was also largely at home. She had studied pure maths at Oxford and we managed to provide mental stimulation for each other. Our boys are still great friends and, about fifteen years later, we are still in regular contact.

I had a three-year maternity leave before returning to part-time temporary roles – often several at the same time, including a lecturer role (maternity cover), work teaching and marking on UG and PG Psychology courses and working as a research fellow on several different projects, in order to avoid working through the school holidays! The only regular support I had was from my NCT friend. In the holidays, we would regularly look after each other's children to allow the other to work. I learned to be pretty self-reliant and how to pull all-nighters in my thirties, staying up to mark assignments and write lectures and conference papers instead of socialising.

While doing these temporary roles, I taught lots of statistics and research methods and was struck by how many of the adults I was working with were scared of maths. They didn't enjoy it and felt it was something they could never be good at. I was looking for an employment solution ... something that I could do as a single parent, with no family around to help with the holidays and primary teaching seemed like the obvious choice. I had carried out lots of research in schools so I wasn't worried about managing behaviour and I knew I could teach. Plus, after my experiences, I knew I wanted to focus on primary rather than secondary, as I wanted to influence children before they had decided maths was not for them.

The training experience was hard, as it is for everyone! I was a single parent but maintained positive interactions with my son's dad who took him to school in the mornings. Having emergency surgery for appendicitis in week three put everything else into perspective though!

I used to find the evenings challenging; juggling life, leaving early enough to collect my son from after-school club, then organising homework, dinner, marking, bath and bedtime routines and then finishing any marking. I slowly increased the responsibility I had for my class and the children and their parents welcomed me back with open arms after my time in a second placement school. I think this was the thing that really kept me going – the relationships with the children and the trust that their parents placed in me. A change in SLT at Christmas added to the challenge and a visit from Ofsted in May completed the excitement.

I have a son who is autistic. This makes me value relationships with parents more than I perhaps otherwise would have. I know the value of a teacher who knows your child, who sees their strengths and not just the challenge they bring. I know the feeling of being a parent who has to be advocate as well as mum and I believe that working with parents as a team to support a child to achieve the best outcomes is the standard we should aim for.

I believe that being a teacher makes me a more effective advocate for my son; it allows me to be solution focused because I know more about what's possible and likely. I think because I have needed to advocate for my son, I am more understanding of the emotional and practical responses of those who are parents to the children I teach. I come from a place of valuing diversity, rather than labelling disorder; I focus on finding strengths and abilities and building on them.

I have learnt so many lessons from my time lecturing and doing research jobs. They have made me evidence focused and I am able to confidently access and critique research papers – this is so important in a world where we are bombarded with conflicting educational research. Speaking at international conferences and interacting with well-known researchers helped my confidence and has made me determined to stand by my beliefs and convictions.

Importantly, my experiences teaching adults, who were frequently older than me, made me realise that you don't have to be old to be good at something and to be able to help someone else. I started teaching as a trainee and as an NQT with the expectation that I would be valued and heard. I was not the finished product, I am still not the finished product, but I see teaching as a journey of continual improvement, constantly learning and adapting. The developmental nature of my HE teaching journey set my expectations for my primary teaching journey. I will get things right, I will get things wrong, I will learn and improve. My thoughts, experiences and individuality will be valued. I will be helped and supported when needed and I will be encouraged and enabled to help and support others. For the most part, my expectations have been met.

I am the kind of teacher who believes all have the potential to learn and with appropriate scaffolding, all can make progress. I don't believe in non-negotiables like three-part lessons or three-way differentiation. I think we need to know our pupils, support them and ensure that our own behaviours do not leave children feeling that they are less able than their peers.

Luke Haisell

I was born and raised in a Kentish seaside town called Hythe, the son of a fisherman – an age-old occupation which is very different from where I have ended up. However, my dad's job has taught me so much that I apply to the classroom every day: hard work pays off; love what you do; an enriching job is not only 9-5; and to reflect on what you do and amend it for the greatest success.

At the age of eleven, I was not 'smart' enough to pass the Kent test (a test that allows you to apply for a grammar school), so I went to my local non-selective secondary school. This decision empowered me, enabling me to flourish. This experience would later become part of my very fabric; I even went back to teach at the school I attended. I wanted to enable others like me, from the same community, to have the same chances that my secondary school gave to me.

Teaching is a multifaceted, varied and wholly enriching career. In what other profession can you take risks, be independent, be creative, foster others' success, enable people to push themselves beyond their background and context, be a therapist, be a motivational speaker, be an analyst, be a strategic thinker, be an academic, a mentor, build communities, and help families? Becoming a teacher bucked the family fisherman history; a path which historically I should have followed. Although I felt sad that I was not following in the footsteps of my family, my dad was far from sad – instead, he saw this as a positive move.

My dad wanted me to create a life of my own, to do well, be happy and successful, from whichever path that might be. My family's support, love and care was instrumental in allowing me to study hard whilst my parents cooked dinner, drove me to revision sessions, paid for my revision books, etc. They went above and beyond to ensure that I had a safe and happy upbringing. As a result of this, I was the first generation to go to university in the family and graduation day was an extremely proud and poignant moment for both my parents and me.

As with many teachers, it often takes a teacher to inspire a teacher. The teacher which inspired me was Mrs Trevelyan, my English teacher. Her love of words, literature, history and culture ignited a passion in this fisherman's son. Mrs Trevelyan taught me the exciting and diverse nature of the subject and how through the pages of a novel you can learn science, geography, religion, sociology, art or even linguistics. I was mesmerised by Mrs Trevelyan's articulacy and passion; I wanted to lead a similar life, sharing in the experiences of a novel and exploring different ideas, given that people approach the subject from their own contexts and placing their own experiences on their understanding of a text.

Growing up, I had always struggled with my weight and I eventually ended up hitting 21 stone, while I was studying for my A-levels. At school, I was never bullied, a testament to the positive and happy secondary school I attended. However, my own self-doubt and lack of social confidence was the greatest bully. At university I decided that I wanted more self-confidence and to improve my mental health. Likewise, the fear of entering the classroom with a lack of self-confidence daunted me. I set about losing the weight, which totalled to an eventual loss of nine stone. The process was hard and challenging with multiple ups and downs.

I draw on these lessons and this journey regularly in my teaching and it has shaped me as an educator in not just the physical sense! Through sharing my story, I can highlight the importance of tenacity and teach the acceptance of difference. It is also key to talk about having a healthy food relationship and to discuss the links between an active body and an active mind. But most importantly, I understand how difficult it can be to have confidence and self-esteem. From the weight loss journey I went on, I feel I am a compassionate teacher with an anecdotal understanding of inner strength, personal goals and resilience – something which we all try to instil in the young people we teach. I have corridor-mentored a number of students who ask about how I lost the weight and reasons for doing it. As a result, they have lost weight and more importantly started to feel better and more confident about themselves. My weight experience has developed my understanding and value of self-confidence, the relationship between mental wellbeing and success, an understanding of resilience which gives me a unique perspective to teach from.

Outside of my professional life, I enjoy exercise including weight training classes, running and dance related exercise; there is nothing better than the feeling after a class that you have achieved something great. To relax and unwind, I enjoy singing, playing the piano and cooking with my soon-to-be wife. Together, we love going on walks and visiting coffee shops to enjoy a brew and some cake! Our favourite spot of an evening is to sit on Hythe beach, overlooking my dad's boat and the English Channel, with a cup of tea to chat about our days.

But as a teacher, I define myself principally as a learner; I model the pursuit of knowledge. It is important for pupils to understand that it is okay to make mistakes and how to deal with them effectively. I learn every day from the students I teach. From the way I dress, the way I deal with inconsiderate behaviour, to the way I speak to all colleagues, I strive to model respect, professionalism and kindness. All young people, regardless of background and ability, can improve their life chances and live happy fulfilling lives: this is the pedagogical ethos which sits behind everything I do.

Lesley Douglas

I was born in Islington, in 1957, into a working-class family. My parents and grandparents were all interested in education—my dad studied navigation and astronomy at night school—and the arts and history. My grandparents and a tenant lived in the same large Victorian terrace and we knew virtually all the families in the street. It was a very lively household and Islington was not the 'posh' area it is now!

My dad taught me and my younger sisters to swim and regularly took us into the country where we learnt about the environment: the names of trees, flowers, life cycles of frogs, bees... My dad had been sent to live on a farm in Wales during World War 2 and his love for the natural world stems from that time. We always had a holiday, often on the coast camping or caravanning. We all learnt to ride a bike, went horse riding and enjoyed visiting houses and gardens of significance and Longleat Safari.

My mum was always strict, but she was also quite funny – but she insisted on high standards. In her teens she had given up a good clerical job to join the land army and later travelled around the world with friends, which was less common than it is now. In many ways my mum encouraged us all to be independent and myself and both my sisters have gone on to have successful professional careers. I was the first in my family to university, definitely encouraged by my dad's motto, "Everyone deserves a fair crack of the whip!"

Perhaps the biggest influence on me becoming a teacher was my great grandmother, Julia Watson. I never met her, but she was the first literate person in my family. Before Julia, my family had been living in the borders of the dark and light blue section of Shoreditch (poor to chronic) but their circumstances steadily improved in the latter 1890s. This taught me that education and literacy were powerful tools in improving people's lives and aspirations.

I also had the privilege of interacting with a broad range of people – grandparents who worked incredibly hard in the early 1900s and suffered illness and tragedy due to poverty, a cousin who was a prisoner of war in Poland and neighbours who played piano and introduced me to sculpture. I babysat for middle class people, whose homes were full of books and classical music, who went to the ballet and took the time to share their passion with an interested sixteen-year-old. Engaging with such a broad range of people and my own background nudged me towards becoming a teacher.

Of course, like many educators, my own experience with teachers was definitely a factor in my choice to teach. Some teachers I came across were mean and unkind. Fortunately, there were more lovely teachers who shared their enjoyment of learning and went out of their way to help when I struggled. They listened to my problems and took the time to help me think about strategies. It was the humour, the smiles of encouragement that made me want to succeed and carried me through to making appropriate exam choices, which led to a place at the Chelmer Institute.

My favourite teacher was Miss Browning. I can still see her vividly in my mind's eye. She was always calm, interesting and had a way of taking you through every subject without you feeling like a failure if you got it wrong. Miss Jones had a long plait she could sit on. She was the music teacher and was lots of fun. She shared a huge range of music with us and we took part in playing recorders, drums, glockenspiel and giving school performances. If pupils aren't laughing, they are not learning.

Working at Hackney Downs School was a revelation. I started in September 1979 and at 22 years of age, experienced so much.

What happened at Hackney Downs has been well documented by the press. The school was founded in 1876 as The Grocers' Company's School. On its transfer to the London County Council in 1906 the school was renamed Hackney Downs School. It was once a prestigious school, with an amazing set of alumni, including Nobel prize-winning playwright Harold Pinter, Steven Berkoff and Lord Levy. Then in 1969, it became a comprehensive school and the intake changed drastically. By the time of its closure, over 70 percent of the boys spoke English as a second language, half came from households with no-one in employment, and half the intake had reading ages of three years below the national average.

In the 1990s, the school made national news because it was described by the then Conservative government as being the 'worst school in Britain.' In 1995, after immense pressure from the government, we were forced to close.

My experiences at Hackney Downs were very different from the dogma being pushed by government. The staff were progressive, very passionate about education and its impact for positive change on young people's lives. The ethos in the school was to support and develop young staff; to enrich them as teachers. I was so fortunate to team teach with experienced teachers who provided me with valuable advice, responding to my teaching with praise when deserved and suggestions for different approaches when lessons did not go as planned. Failing in the classroom was used to help me learn from mistakes and develop strengths, so I felt my own learning and 'teacher evolution' was encouraged and that there was a safety net for when things went wrong.

Of course, not everything was fantastic. Sometimes I felt teaching was not for me and I did think of giving up. It is not easy dealing with pupil difficulties or fully appreciating the (sometimes horrific) backgrounds they came from. But teaching at HDS was more than just education; it was holistic. The school had a very vibrant youth club attached to it. So many brilliant youth workers added to the lives of the young men and women that attended. There were so many activities on offer, from canoeing to trips to the wonderful education centre, Kench Hill, Tenterden. HDS was a lifeline for some pupils. Teachers and pupils worked together; the boys knew their teachers really wanted to help and support them. There were times of conflict, but on the whole, there was a lot of mutual regard and respect.

The politics in Hackney at the time became so turbulent and I don't pretend to completely understand what was going on, but it caused a crisis for the school. The issues around its closure are too complex for me to summarise here and staff were put under a ban with regard to speaking to the press, but once I had taken voluntary redundancy I was freed up and did indeed speak to the BBC.

Going into Hackney Downs and all that happened there was probably the most important experience in my early career as a teacher. To be able to work with Frances Magee, Gordon Gilchrist,

Bernice Cornell, John Hardcastle, Roger Symons, Peter Traves and Betty Hales to name but a few, was an honour. The whole staff were amazing, introducing me to new ideas and developing my practice. John Kemp was Head, Stan Gunter and Harvey Monte Deputies – all three were fantastic practitioners and so willing to share their experiences. To be told you had handled a difficult situation well or to suggest a different approach without a hint that you muffed up, meant you continued to grow and thrive. It was tough but I learned a lot. Despite the difficulties I faced I would still choose HDS if I could go back and do it again.

After HDS was closed I ran away to Africa! Although, you can never really run away. I had friends in Africa who invited me to stay with them and at that time, I felt as though no school would ever want me and that my career was over. If you look at press cuttings, what happened at HDS was being shared by academics, and statisticians and others were re-evaluating the contribution HDS had made to the politics of education. I hoped by leaving the country I could recover in some anonymity.

Africa is such a beautiful country, truly breathtaking. I spent time in Johannesburg, taking quite a long, guided tour into the bush, camping and watching wildlife. I needed to be quiet and calm and it certainly helped. The experience that had most impact was one very starry night lying back and looking and listening. I could see the curvature of space. It helped put events into perspective.

Every issue, event, experience had an impact. I spent almost a year out of the UK, but when my money ran out, I had to come home not knowing if I would get a job. After this experience, I do not take anything for granted, as the rug can be pulled from under you at any time. I learned that there are always lovely people who will help you and there are others who use you for their own means. It is the same everywhere.

Education has the potential to influence a person's future life chances. I always tried to do my best. By listening to children, I learned how to help them. They know what they need and must be included. Some of my best results came out of sharing my planning with the boys I taught. If you can't learn the way I teach, then I will teach the way you learn.

Gwen Mayor
as told by her daughter Deborah Buchanan

My amazing mum Gwen grew up in Great Harwood in Lancashire and met my dad Rodney when she was fourteen. They married when she was twenty-one, at the local Methodist church and moved to Scotland in the early 1970s to set up home in Bridge of Allan. My sister, Esther and I were born later in 1975 and 1977.

My mum taught in many schools within central Scotland but ended up teaching at Dunblane Primary School; she taught there for ten years before her death.

On the 13th March 1996, my mum was teaching her class of five- and six-year olds in the school gym, when gunman Thomas Hamilton entered and opened fire. In less than three minutes, he had killed or wounded almost everybody in the room. He went for the adults first, so his first victim was my mum. She was shot six times and died almost instantly.

On the day she died, it is known that she was found in a position where she was shielding some of the pupils in her class as best as she could. I know it would have been her first instinct to protect them. I get solace in some form, from knowing she is still looking after them, the sixteen children who died alongside her that day.

At the time of the shooting, I was only nineteen and was studying at the University of North London. I had last seen my mum three months before and our relationship had always been special. We wrote letters and spoke on the phone and loved going shopping when she visited me.

I remember hearing about the massacre on the radio, but I couldn't get hold of anyone at home. The police line was engaged, and I began to worry that my mum was involved but I tried to remain calm and not imagine the worst. But when my dad called to break the news that mum had been killed, it didn't seem real at first. It was only when I got the next flight home that the enormity of the situation hit me, and I burst into tears.

It was in the weeks after, that I really struggled to cope with the loss. How could we carry on as normal? It felt so unfair. We were devastated by her loss and we feel it every day, especially when I look at my own children and know that my mum wasn't there to meet them or give me advice.

She was awarded the Queen's Commendation for Bravery posthumously in 1997 and was also named Scotswoman of the Year for her outstanding bravery and tremendous courage. I am so proud of her.

Some things I can tell you about my mum is how creative a person she was and how she transferred this into her classroom. She inspired and enthused the pupils she taught with her imagination, making learning fun and visual. She also used her love of music, particularly the piano, in her teaching. This has led to the Gwen Mayor Trust being set up in her name by her union, the EIS, due to her bravery and commitment to teaching. Each year, the trust awards monies to primary school projects to help fund projects connected with the subjects she loved such as the arts, music and culture. I am on the board of trustees and I know she would be so proud of this lasting legacy, which benefits children in Scotland's primary schools.

She was vibrant, elegant, vivacious, charming and beautiful. These were the attributes that were also encompassed in a rose created in her name by Cockers, which unfortunately is no longer available. But when it was, money from sales of the roses went towards the EIS trust in her name.

Today I grieve for the loss of the mum I should have had, the gran my children should have known. Her being able to watch her daughters grow up and become adults she would have been proud of, even being at our weddings. I am proud of the teacher she was and the granny I know she would have been.

Maureen McDevitt

When I was six years old, I wanted to become a nun and I became consumed with collecting money so I could buy "mission babies." My plan was to name them Jesus, Mary and Joseph. It is funny to think back on it now but the experience of being taught by nuns helped lay the foundation for my career. I had a desire to help improve society through charity and saw the nuns as role models. Although, I no longer wish to buy 'mission babies', for obvious ethical reasons!

Like many teachers, I was inspired by some fantastic educators throughout my academic career. I wanted to be in a position to use literature to inspire students that were like me: quiet and troubled.

The journey has not been easy and has always been filled with self-doubt. I grew up in poverty in Philadelphia, living in a three-room apartment with my mother. She was an alcoholic but worked two jobs so that I could attend Catholic school. I am the first person in my family to attend and finish university – a problematic childhood fuelled my desire to use education as a way out.

Currently, I am a Freelance Educator for the National Holocaust Centre and am completing my MRes in Holocaust Studies at NTU. My research is looking at whether graphic novels can be used to teach the Holocaust in religious education. But it has been a long and varied journey to get here. I have had roughly twenty-three different jobs leading up to my career as a teacher, everything from working as a clown to a Starbucks barista...

I even nearly became a Philadelphia Police Officer. I scored very highly on the entrance test but bizarrely, was not called to attend the orientation. It transpired that a group of women were being discriminated against, because a group of men scored lower and received their acceptance into orientation. I became part of a class action suit against the City of Philadelphia. After going through this ordeal, I eventually received my letter to attend orientation to Police Academy Training. But I was so put off by the experience, I decided to go back to university and get my teaching degree. I had witnessed the injustices of the world and thought I could make much more of an impact as a teacher.

My first teaching job was in the inner city of Philadelphia and I was hired as a drama teacher at a middle school. I lasted six and a half days in that school. On one of the days, I had students asking me to teach them how to read and others who were kept back so often they were the oldest in the class. The students were living in abject poverty and many were dabbling in prostitution or were involved with drugs. I think growing up with an alcoholic mother helped me to be more sensitive to the factors hindering students' academic or social progress, but I had never witnessed such social problems as I saw in that school.

On my last day, a student tried to crawl out of a second-floor window. At home that night, I decided that I was not cut out for teaching. The demands were too much and I could not help the students in the way that I wanted to. I resigned from my first job after less than a week.

However, it was not long before I was lured back into the classroom through a temporary opportunity to teach in my old grade school. Teaching amongst the teachers who had shaped me early on was slightly daunting.

The events of 9/11 proved to be the catalyst for a monumental change in the life of my family. I had recently started teaching in my dream school. Nazareth Academy Catholic High School was like the one I attended as a teen and run by the same sisters who had taught me my whole life. This teaching job felt like a perfect fit. On 9/11, I was teaching when there was an announcement by the principle on the PA system which informed everyone of a plane hitting one of the towers in the World Trade Center. Many of the students had parents who worked in NYC and were in Manhattan on the day. The students began to hold hands and pray. What followed was sheer panic from the students. Soon after, all of the schools in the city were closing early and dismissal was immediate. Students scrambled to get out of school and go home. One student saw me waiting for the bus so that I could pick up my daughter from daycare, as it was closing immediately. The student stopped her car and told me to get in so she could drive me home. The student did not know me but the events of the morning provided a sense of urgency for all of us to get home. In the chaos of the day, no one knew what was going on or whether we were at war. Seeing the panic on the faces of the students on that day and the events that followed, was the catalyst for eventually moving to England. I wanted my daughter to have a happy childhood, free from the fears promoted in America. I felt that we could have a better life in England than we could in America so we started the process to emigrate.

When I moved to England in 2003, my husband at the time decided to end the marriage. I had only left my country and moved to the other side of the world with our four-year-old daughter a year ago. I had to decide whether to go back to Philadelphia or carve out a life as a single mother in a foreign country with very little support and no family. It was so incredibly hard to continue my teaching career in England as a single parent and being foreign in a school which was very insular.

In hindsight, these experiences have helped make me more resilient and empowered me to cope with the changing demands in the UK education system. I decided to move subject disciplines, from English to RE as I believed that I could have an impact on children in a way I did not believe was possible strictly teaching English. RE teachers need to have a certain fight in them because there can be so many factors which make teaching or leading the subject so difficult. RE teachers typically teach a higher volume of students in less instructional time than other core subjects. The subject is not usually valued by students or staff, as students do not feel like the subject is relevant to them because they are either not religious or do not feel it will help them in their career. Furthermore, staff who do not teach RE use their own experience of being an RE student and make an uninformed judgement on what RE actually is today. Senior management often see RE instructional time as an area that could be used to add more time to other subjects and cut RE curriculum time. So when an RE department is not fully supported by a school, leading the subject is often frustrating.

However, at the heart of teaching RE, is the development of a child's empathy and awareness of their role in the wider community which I so rewarding. It is not always easy, but the tough times have helped me to find ways of helping students learn, whilst not being so quick to give up like I did in my first teaching job.

Bizarrely, Ofsted called me "wildly exciting" and I am not so sure whether that is a good thing! I am an extremely creative teacher (I actually wanted to be an art teacher and my father talked me out of it!) and I have an indefatigable approach to making RE engaging and challenging.

I have been fortunate to teach some amazing students. One of my students brought in her Holocaust assessment, which was in the form of a guitar made of cardboard. She struggled with fixing the guitar strings. When I asked her what she was doing, she said, "I just want my work to mean something." Her words have stuck with me as I try to think about what the work I set, or the lessons I teach, mean for all of my students.

Sadly, some students can be apathetic about their work. In one class, the majority of the students were submitting work which did not meet the standard I expected or the quality of work they were capable of doing in RE. I created large Taco Bell sauces to display on the wall. Each sauce had the level of effort the students could use as their target for effort in their work. For example, 'Diablo' hot sauce was the maximum amount of effort where the students had pushed themselves to go beyond being complacent with submitting below standard work. If their work met the criteria, I made paper tacos and placed their names on individual tacos. In a short amount of time, the quality of work improved and students were keen to get on the 'Taco About RE Success' wall. Little successes in the classroom, whether it be silly paper tacos on the wall, or students just wanting to find meaning in their work, sustains my love of teaching.

My philosophy comes from a line from Toni Morrison's *Beloved*: "You your best thing, Sethe. You are." This line captures my belief that what we do in the classroom can help students see that *they* are their best thing. Teenagers often do not have the self-confidence or the resilience they need in high school. I like to think that my subject helps build skills that my students need for their lives beyond high school and if I can help them see how amazing they are, then I am happy!

James Atkin

My name is Mr Atkin (but most of my pupils call me Sir). I'm a secondary school teacher at a mid-size school in North Yorkshire in the UK. In a previous life, I was an international popstar who toured the world, had a number one single in the US, was awarded platinum discs for record sales and was nominated for an Ivor Novella song-writing award. My band was called EMF and I was the lead singer.

I did some pretty grim menial jobs the first few years after leaving school, one in an ice cream factory, another in a Xerox photocopying factory. Sadly, leaving school with no qualifications meant this was the only real employment on offer to me in the area I grew up in. It became apparent that many of the people working in these factories had arrived as young people similar to myself and just simply stayed employed there for years, sometimes until they retired. The one thing this experience gave me was a drive to break away from this environment.

I escaped the small town where I lived and managed to move to London, where I got a job in a 'Turkish baths' sauna. This was an eye opener, as it was the first time I'd really mixed with and worked alongside people from different cultures. I came away from this working experience having learnt that the world is a very interesting place, and that diversity, whether it is multiculturalism, accepting different religious beliefs or different sexualities or even those who come from economic backgrounds, is something to embrace and something that enriches your life.

The seeds of EMF the band were planted during my time at school, as myself and all but one of the members of EMF attended the same school. We spent most weekends rehearsing and practicing in old barns or church halls, and we eventually started gigging whilst in our final year of school. It was a time when people turned a blind eye to underage drinking, particularly in the rural area where we grew up. We slowly built a following of local fans and honed our craft. Then in late 1989, we were offered a record deal by EMI and put on the road to success. This was a slog, lots of travelling up and down the country in a transit van and crashing in cheap hotels. We released our first single 'Unbelievable' in 1990 and the song entered the UK charts and then the US charts. A lot of the time, we were on tour travelling the world and visiting amazing countries such as Mexico and Australia. One of my most memorable experiences was being arrested at gunpoint in Louisiana and being escorted off a plane before take-off from Brazil, for stealing the captain's hat!

Life was a rollercoaster of fun and partying. The partying sadly came to end when we lost our bass player and best friend Zak Foley, due to a drugs overdose. I have no real regrets and I wouldn't necessarily do anything differently I guess, apart from perhaps not blowing so much money on partying; I could have been a little more sensible, but it was a riot and a definitely an experience.

As my pop career inevitably waned, I decided to quit London and move to the North of England, to a little quiet village in the Yorkshire Dales. Life had been a whirlwind up to this point for so many years and it felt like a change was due.

Life was strange and surprisingly unfulfilling with no real job, career, structure or purpose. Initially, I did envisage having a quiet life and retiring. I was thirty-eight at this stage! I soon realized I needed to do something. I was getting bored and life seemed a bit aimless and worthless.

I went and volunteered at an urban arts centre in the city of Bradford, teaching young people who were struggling and were disengaged with the mainstream school system. I showed them how to DJ and produce records. I absolutely loved this experience and the thought entered my head – 'Well maybe I could become a teacher?'

At this point I had no qualifications and was fairly unemployable – what do old popstars do? I enrolled to do a teaching degree at Huddersfield University and they thankfully allowed me to do this because of my professional musician background; whilst on the course, I had to take my GCSE Maths and English. I did pass, but it took a lot of hard work and dedication. I was in my forties when I finally passed, and I sometimes let this slip to my GCSE students I teach now.

But I didn't find teaching easy at first. I was asked by a teacher at a local secondary school to come and help with some GCSE music composition pieces and she asked if I wanted to take a couple of classes. I did a few lessons and discovered it wasn't for me – I was clueless about how to teach and how to manage a class numbering twenty-eight disruptive Year 9s. I went and visited the school Headmaster and told him I was giving up. The headmaster persuaded me to give it another shot, offering me loads of support.

Over the years I've gone from taking those few initial lessons to being a full-time teacher who now has many roles within the school, including being a form teacher, pastoral care, teaching many subjects that are not my primary specialism (I'm a music teacher officially) and the dreaded playground duties, where I endlessly chase kids around and warn them about the perils of smoking.

The fact I was a popstar in EMF is not on my students' radar and has no relevance to them really. Occasionally a song might pop up on an advert or film, but other than that it was way over a lifetime ago for them. Parents Evenings did use to be interesting though, with parents making their way towards me for autographs!

But it's not just my former career that has influenced me as a teacher. I have a young family member who has been diagnosed with autism and this has been a major learning curve for our family. It has made me very aware of teaching students who are on the spectrum and how important it is to implement certain teaching techniques to aid their learning. They can also have mental health issues and severe anxiety, resulting in them struggling at times. The personal experience of this has definitely helped shape my approach to teaching in the classroom. I now hope I'm not too quick to judge a student's actions or behaviours without questioning the circumstances first.

It has taken me quite a few years to find my style – initially I struggled with being an authoritarian type figure, especially as this was everything I stood against in my early life. I'm a big fan of letting students develop their creativity through nurturing and exploring ideas, something that schools sometimes sidestep. I do follow Bloom's Taxonomy and have found this invaluable throughout my twelve years of teaching. There is a reason that certain ideologies are vital and proven: SMART objectives, differentiation, continued professional development, scaffolding questions, targeted open-ended questioning, etc. They all make us better teachers and improve learning for our young people.

Mostly, my years as a music star taught me not to be too serious. I always like to make sure the pupils have fun. I do drop in the odd rock 'n' roll story every now and again, but am careful to edit the content in it, or else I'm sure I'd get sacked.

I'm also a firm believer in Kolb's Experiential Learning Theory. This seems to work well within my own specialism, as it can be very subjective judging and assessing music, in particular performance and composition.

As far as my ethos goes, I keep it relaxed. The student's welfare and happiness is way more important to me than grades and results.

Katharine Birbalsingh

I was born in Auckland, New Zealand but grew up for the most part in Canada. Both of my parents are immigrants. My mum was a nurse from Jamaica and my father is of Indo-Guyanese descent and was a lecturer at university.

I grew up mostly in Toronto but moved to the UK at age fifteen, for my father's job. When my family returned to Canada, I stayed in England.

I went to Oxford University and studied French and philosophy at New College. I was a typical state school kid. As a result, when I arrived at Oxford, I was really far behind my peers; all of these private school kids were so much better educated than I was. I had to work hard to catch up.

When the time came to figure out what to do after university, firms like McKinsey and Price and Waterhouse Cooper would come to

Oxford, give us a glass of wine and try to seduce us with a certain lifestyle. But it didn't feel right for me. I didn't want to do any of that... I wanted to help change the world for the better!

I was part of a group of black students who would go and visit inner city schools in London, Birmingham and Manchester and tell the students, "If I am okay at Oxford, then you can think about applying too." Historically, many black kids wouldn't even consider applying to places like Oxford because they had this perception that it was just for posh white kids. I would hear the pupils saying negative things upon my arrival, but then they would change their minds. I found that my talks would inspire some pupils to apply to Oxbridge and I really felt like I was making a difference; it was then that I knew teaching was for me.

I was always very open to progressive ideas in education. I was just like any other PGCE student and I did as I was told. That meant using progressive teaching methods. But over time I learned that the more progressive methods didn't deliver the same quality of learning as the more traditional methods. Through trial and error during my career, I changed my mind. I am not ideological about it. I just try stuff out and if it works, I go with it. Same thing now at Michaela – I do what works when running the school. That's why we are able to make decisions that are radically different to the norm. I don't do things just because they have always been done.

A lot of my expectations about life come from my father, who was a man of the 'Left.' He had friends who were self-proclaimed Communists! He was a typical immigrant in his mentality: he believed in hard work, perseverance and determination. So, I was brought up in a household where small 'c' Conservative values were in abundance. Take note: it is possible for Lefties to have small 'c' Conservative values! My parents brought me up immersed in the values of hard work and personal responsibility.

We established Michaela Community School as a free school in September 2014 and we set the school up in a converted office block, which had been converted before we arrived into an FE college. We were a group of teachers and people interested in education and we named the school after my old colleague, Michaela Emanus, who sadly died of cancer in 2011. She believed in rigour and old-fashioned values, in kids being allowed to be kids and adults being role models who lead the way. She would have been so proud of the school and everything we have achieved.

In teaching, I have met lots of kids like me. Only last week I had a conversation with a girl in the Sixth Form who wouldn't believe she could get to Oxford because she was black. She had all of these worries about whether they would want her and how she would survive. But I could talk about my own experiences there and tell her that she was wrong but that I understood why she had these worries, because I had them too.

Then there are those conversations with other pupils, about feeling that you're not good enough – and I very much know what that feels like. There were many times at Oxford when I felt inadequate. I know what it is like to feel like you're stupid, that there must be something wrong with you. I know what it is like to feel like you are never going to catch up with everyone else. Perhaps that's why throughout my career, I always enjoyed the bottom sets most. I loved those little bottom set Year 7s, trying to teach them enough so that they might feel clever in the world.

I also know what it is like to feel like you don't have any friends. When I was at school, I was a bit of a nerd and I worked hard, so I wasn't very popular. I was the only black girl in a white school in the 1980s, so I wasn't really girlfriend material: boys tended to view me as an alien – or a giraffe. I was definitely not cool. I was black and a nerd and was just so different. They would call us names in those days, like 'paki' or 'coon' make fun of my "chocolate-covered" face. So, I know what it is like to feel like you are on the outside looking in all of the time. Again, as a teacher throughout my career, maybe this is why I loved being in my classroom at lunch or break time, so that the gay kids, the nerdy kids or the kids who didn't have many friends could hang out in my room and feel safe, away from the social nightmare of the yard or the corridors.

Some of the girls I have taught over the years have spoken to me about their worries about how they're not pretty enough, not light-skinned enough, not thin enough. As a kid, I was black, tall, skinny and nerdy and so I definitely know what it's like to feel like one isn't pretty, or admired, or wanted. For years, people would ask if I was a boy or a girl because my mother cut my hair really short. It was too 'black' (afro mixed) and she got tired of combing it. My life was ruined for years because of it!

I think it's important for children to know that we have been through tough times too and that things will change over a lifetime. It may seem like school is the whole world right now because you are fourteen and it seems like boys are never going to fancy you, but they will one day! And one day the things that matter now aren't going to matter so much in the future. You just have to wait a little while, that's all. I promise.

I would never have imagined the tough days I had as a kid would be of use later on, but in life, you never know what lies around the corner. I suppose that's part of my motivation to make Michaela a safe school where bullying doesn't exist. I know what it is like to be a victim of a school culture where anything goes. And I wouldn't wish that on anyone.

Hugh Ogilvie

I was a lawyer between 1993 and 2015, although only fully qualified from the end of 1995. I worked initially in the commercial sector, then moved to become a Criminal Defence Lawyer, working initially in North East London, East London, Enfield Town and latterly, Devon.

I realised that I wasn't being fulfilled by my occupation as a criminal defence lawyer and advocate at the courts. I had lost my inspiration and felt both directionless and disaffected with my profession. I only really became a lawyer because that was what was expected, and I was 'pushed' in that direction. My view on teaching was that it was an honourable profession and I always reflected upon my teachers as people to be respected and looked up to, as well as those who inspired me and made me want to learn and challenge myself. Both of my parents were teachers, although my father had stopped teaching several years before I started at university.

Dissatisfied with my job, I decided to retrain as a teacher as I had a burning desire to make more of a difference than I was doing in my current role and I wanted to try and pay back the influence and passion that I witnessed in my own teachers at secondary school. Moreover, I had spent a lot of time writing about music and poetry and I had always wanted to be creative with words throughout my working life; I felt that I could put this to effective use in the teaching profession. I also felt relatively well-placed due to my experiences at the 'coal face' of publicly funded legal aid work, dealing with individuals from a very wide variety of backgrounds in generally stressful circumstances.

During my time as a lawyer, I represented clients as young as ten years old and up to the age of eighty, for offences as seemingly trivial as possession of cannabis to the very serious, such as murder and rape. The approach I took was objective and evidence-based, which allowed me to look at each case dispassionately and deal with issues arising in a timely and efficient manner. It also allowed me to develop rich interpersonal and communication skills both at the police station and in the courtroom. I learnt to quickly gain the trust of every new client so that they could go along with my considered advice and make the right decision for themselves. Inevitably, for some of these cases, I had to deal with people in often highly emotional situations, so it was important to be able to maintain a clear head at all times and keep control, to enable the most favourable outcomes.

As I said before, I wanted a new and refreshing challenge, which would allow me to extend my love of learning as a lifelong concept.

Now, I am currently in my fourth year of teaching in a state secondary school. My subject is English, and I teach from Key Stage 3, all the way up to Key Stage 5. I trained at Marjon University in Plymouth, then completed my first two years of teaching in

Exeter, before moving to Oxfordshire. I have just started my second year at a state-funded school, which is currently in 'Requires Improvement.' There are challenges about convincing parents that your school is the best school for their child, when you are in direct competition with other schools in the area that are either 'Good' or 'Outstanding.' You are aware that, for some disadvantaged and SEND students, they may not be getting the best deal throughout the school which is holding them back. Behaviour is generally good, but challenges do remain. Exam results have been worse than the previous year and, for the minority subjects, a three-year GCSE curriculum now has to be reduced to two years under the new Ofsted framework, which is causing a fair degree of stress and anxiety. We have also had several recent changes in SLT within the school, which has led to rapid change and a feeling of instability amongst the staff body.

However, with over twenty-two years as a lawyer and solicitor, I think my experience allows me to adapt to challenge and think logically in different and difficult situations. I am more likely to be non-judgmental towards students and other colleagues in light of the depth of my previous experience, after being involved in many challenging cases that required care and sensitivity. I am objective in my approach, but I allow my subjective attitude towards the texts I teach to emerge through my teaching.

I also believe I have learnt a great deal from my initial struggles with getting to grips with the fundamentals of teaching – this was both helped and hindered to some extent by my previous experiences in the private sector and a very different, less collegiate approach. What I mean is that, as a lawyer, you rely on obtaining new work from the duty police station and court schemes – you work, very much, as an individual with no additional support which can make you feel quite vulnerable at times, since you are judged – to an extent – upon your results and how you deal with each case and the outcome for the client. You might have clients who decide to transfer their representation and you have to be on your guard for this. There is no teamwork as such – you have a department but you are making money for the firm you work for and your time is billable, unlike as a teacher; this increases the pressure and you cannot really relax.

As my own teaching practice has improved, I have found that Continuous Professional Development and collaborating with other teachers has helped to shape my open-minded outlook on my pedagogy and the skills that I continue to use and acquire on a daily basis. Like when I was failing early on in my new career, I was able to draw on reserves of resilience to help me cope with challenge and improve my chances, as well as the support I received from fellow professionals. This interest in teaching and learning has led to me recently starting blogging with the moniker 'Reflection Eternal.' The blog focuses on book reviews, personal experiences and thoughts and ideas about education.

I believe that teaching my subject is a privilege and that I have a genuine responsibility to communicate my passion for English, in order to seek to inspire every student in my care to want to succeed and feel curious about the world of fiction, non-fiction, plays, poetry, speaking and listening, music and film. It helps that I have a particular passion for hip hop and jazz music and adore films of all genres – especially by Tarantino, Scorsese, Shane Meadows, Coppola and modern female film directors such as Lynne Ramsay, Andrea Arnold, Jane Campion and Kathryn Bigelow.

I believe that every child can achieve but that it requires a level of commitment and resilience to succeed. I believe that teaching should combine concepts and ideas with the necessary skills and tools to enable students to transform into independent and creative thinkers, who care about their own education, individual progress and place in the world. To foster, I have started up a Key Stage 5 debating club and will be involved as a volunteer with the Duke of Edinburgh awards scheme.

As the father of a Year 11 boy myself, I want the students I teach to develop a love for the subject, to take proper risks, adopt the mantle of hunger for new knowledge and to want to transform that knowledge into something meaningful for each of them. Ultimately, my goal is for them to become fully literate, with enquiring minds and the ability to embrace an ideology of lifelong, limitless learning ability. They should never stand still but should have the powerful need and ambition to reach further beyond structures placed upon them by society, social mobility, or indeed, themselves.

Victoria Hewett

It seems like a bit of a mouthful but I'm a geography trained teacher with experience of teaching geography, history, religious studies, citizenship, environmental science and ICT. I'm currently Subject Leader for geography and environmental systems and societies at Tonbridge Grammar School, where I have been since September 2016. Previously I was Head of Humanities at a free school in Kent.

My road to teaching was pretty direct, as before teaching, I undertook a BSc in geography at the University of Wales, Aberystwyth – as it was called at the time – now known as Aberystwyth University. During and after my time there, I worked at the Centre for Alternative Technology. It was here I decided to enter into education, be it environmental education.

Towards the end of my degree and for a year after I worked three different jobs: two at the Centre for Alternative Technology and the others were simply bar work. However, after that, my partner and I were forced to move to the South East due to poor health in the family. Whilst in the South East, I sought experience in environmental education and ended up doing an unpaid internship with Global Action Plan whilst working in a bar to cover the cost of living.

I undertook a PGCE, not because I wanted to be a teacher (although I had when I'd been younger) but because I wanted to work in Environmental Education. I'd been inspired to involve myself in education whilst I worked at the Centre for Alternative Technology. One day a school group had arrived from Birmingham and one of the boys had been incredibly excited. He said, "I've just seen a real-life cow and it wasn't in a McDonald's cheeseburger." It was this point I knew I wanted to work with young people, to educate them about the world in which they lived and their role in managing and conserving it.

However, whilst looking for jobs in the sector I found that most required a PGCE or similar teaching qualification. Yet, I found that I really enjoyed being in the classroom and didn't want to leave it. I realised I could have greater impact here than I could working with schools.

Eight years down the line and I'm still in the classroom.

Despite not having any formal classroom experience, the fast-paced nature of bar work surprisingly set me up for the speedy pace of classroom teaching, not to mention the need to juggle a range of tasks and challenges at the same time. It also helped with dealing with 'unwelcome' behaviour in the classroom or from parents, whilst my experience in the environmental sector developed my understanding and enthusiasm for all things geography and sustainability.

But it's fair to say that teaching has been a rollercoaster for me, right from the training year. Yet every challenge and experience has shaped the teacher I am today.

In April 2014, I started at a new school, in my fourth year of teaching. It seemed like the perfect school for me, a free school set up by a land-based colleague which aimed to have sustainability at its heart. Unfortunately, it turned out to be more of a nightmare. The school had only opened in September 2013 and everything needed devising and setting up. However, the workload never faltered, it never eased and despite asking for help in Spring 2015, little support was there. The workload continued and by the penultimate date before Easter 2016, I broke. I burst into tears in front of a class because I'd had enough of the behaviour and the impact on learning, particularly for those that wanted to learn.

The response was merely "Tomorrow will be okay; they'll forget about it quick enough. See you in the morning." Along with a referral to Occupational Health.

It wasn't enough. I returned to work after the Easter break and couldn't enter my classroom. The panic struck; I couldn't breathe, I couldn't move. I sat down outside my classroom and started crying. Yet somehow, I managed to pick myself up off the ground (literally) and make my way inside. At which point when I was asked if I was okay, I simply cried. The tears didn't stop for what felt like hours. I went home. I didn't return for some three weeks and then that was only because I was "encouraged".

During my time off I applied for another job; I gave myself the ultimatum that I'd give one more school a try before leaving the profession but if it didn't work out, I'd know that teaching wasn't for me. I got the job and whilst I worried it would be more of the same, it got me through the last two terms.

I went on antidepressants. I went to work, did my job and tried to leave as early as possible. I stopped putting my everything into a place that had taken so much from me for two years. Despite not wanting to go in, knowing I was leaving got me through each day.

That experience though, as hard as it was, changed the teacher I'd become.

My understanding of mental health has changed and consequently, so has my approach to staff and students. I openly talk about my experiences. I happily show that it is possible to reach rock bottom and recover but also that there are times when you are not okay and that is okay.

It also changed the way I teach. I opt for simplicity and clear focus, supporting students through scaffolding rather than differentiation and feedback, not marking. I've learnt to plan backwards and to design learning differently to how I'd been taught. My practice is influenced by research, evidence and active reflection.

When I first started to talk openly about my experiences, I thought it might help one or two others who felt like they were in similar positions. I never thought it would open the number of doors it has: I was headhunted to write a book, interviewed on BBC Breakfast, had appearances on local and national BBC and ITV news, later becoming an ambassador for the Education Support Partnership, talking at events and conferences ... the list goes on. I've been able to help far more than the one or two I set out to, and that's a real privilege.

I'll happily talk about my experiences with colleagues and friends when they need it too. I am always open to sharing what helped me, how they can help themselves and to show them that burnout doesn't have to be the end of their time in the profession. I've had several colleagues in my current workplace come to me for support and guidance; thankfully we work in a school that is supportive, so my first bit of advice is "talk to your line manager". After that I just listen, and let them get things off their chest before looking for solutions together to help them to reduce and manage their workload more effectively.

As a teacher my ethos centres around my drive to create knowledgeable, responsible global citizens. Everything I teach them works towards social, economic and environmental sustainability for them and the world around them. I'm teaching them to develop as independent learners, providing them with the support and scaffolds they need to get there over time.

Penny Rabiger

I was born and raised in London by my single parent mother. I read social anthropology at Sussex University and then, as an attempt to explore different ways of collaborative living, I ended up travelling for a year in the Middle East and spending the next decade living and teaching, somewhat accidentally, in Jerusalem.

I had a terrible time at school and felt that I might be able to do a better job at reaching students in a more humane and engaged way. I always loved working with children and being creative, so it seemed a natural fit for me to train to be a teacher. I had also worked from age 16 to 24 running summer playschemes and was a supervisor across four sites by the time I was 18. This experience had stayed with me and influenced me to take my next step.

Although the original plan before I went travelling was to do a PGCE at Goldsmiths in London, I did it in Israel and specialised in democratic and alternative education, teaching for four years in the first school to integrate religious and non-religious children in the same classroom. Then I spent seven years in a high school for the performing arts as a form tutor, English and art teacher. During this time, I completed my Masters in Education through Leeds University. The settings I worked in were local state schools, so I also became bi-lingual in Hebrew – out of necessity.

As a teacher and form tutor, I was really interested in being able to reach out to and understand every child. No matter how quiet and well-behaved, or disruptive and rude, I knew that every child has a story and every child wants to be seen, appreciated and nurtured. My own childhood was not happy, and I felt school didn't add anything positive but rather punished me for acting out the distress of the chaos at home. This made me want to relate to children in a way that was respectful, had clear boundaries and that obliged me to connect with each of the children in my classroom.

Relationships are key in the classroom and in any organisation where people work and learn together. As a teacher, I took time to know my students, their families, my colleagues, the ethos of the school and so on. I spent time leading on the co-creation of the learning culture in the classroom with my students, so that keeping focused is easier, as everyone is on board.

I believe that with clarity of purpose, clear boundaries and mutual respect, there can be a calm, respectful, purposeful and exciting classroom environment. I like to provide space and time for creativity, dialogue and personal expression and I am also disciplined about ensuring that there is structured time for the somewhat 'drier' aspects of learning such as spelling, grammar and things that just need to be understood and memorised.

I believe that everyone is a teacher and you can learn from everyone. One of the things I know about learning from other people is that you often have to separate people out into segments of their personality, to understand them and to gain from them what they are there to teach you. What I mean by this can be illustrated by my experience of growing up, which impacted on my own ability to form relationships and get on at school.

My mum had a childhood filled with horrific abuse and mistreatment. She escaped her family and went to art school and by the early 1960s, had been hanging out with a bohemian crowd of fellow artists. Our family home was filled with paintings by her from this era and today, my siblings and I have her bold and vibrant paintings in our own homes. By the time I came along, she was broken. Two failed marriages behind her, she found herself a single parent of two small children and pregnant with me, trying to hold her demons at bay and build a life for herself and her children. It must have been the most awful of times and while she essentially replicated the abuse, neglect and mistreatment on her own children, we each somehow were able to see beyond, to the person she would have liked to have been. We were always able to see her own small-child self-battling the ghosts of her past that had seized her. We were able to see her as the raging adult, fragile and let down by those that should have protected her, somewhere in the fire and brimstone. And at the same time, we were deeply damaged by her, both physically and emotionally.

By some miracle, while we were small children, my mum built herself a career. It was survival. She had been a stay-at-home mum until my older brother was five but with my dad gone, she had to work. She built on her knowledge as an artist and taught. In the 1970s, she taught basket weaving and sculpture at nursing homes, what were then called 'handicapped centres' and in a unit for 'school-phobic' children. She brought home materials and we all learned to paint, draw, weave, do macramé, plaster-casting, sculpting, lino prints – the works. When she taught us, the irritable, quick to be triggered, lashing out hands, would diminish. She would connect for a moment and her voice and eyes would soften.

Throughout my early secondary school years in the 1980s, my mum trained to be an Art Therapist at evening school while working during the day and running the family home as best she could. She started working at a centre for autistic children and later at a special school, and she became hooked. She read voraciously, and became involved in what would now be deemed as action research, constantly thinking about and writing about art as therapy. She found the personal and professional relationships extremely challenging and often felt alienated and misunderstood by her colleagues. But she was real and intense and absolutely committed to her work with the children as a teacher.

In 2007, I moved back to London with my partner and our small children and left the classroom, landing a job with the government pilot of 'The Key for School Leaders' and later became Director of Business Development. Part of this move was to try and care for my mum, whose health was failing. In 2014, she had a stroke and was in rehab with 24-hour nursing care. She eventually passed away 18 months later.

She had always been a hoarder and clearing out her home was the most visceral and ghastly of tasks. I can only liken it to an archaeological dig—perhaps somewhere like Pompeii—each find throwing up images of a life lived and a disaster that had dashed away the possibilities somehow. Each room contained layers of a life holed up in the same house since the 1960s.

In one room, she stored everything from her art teacher and art therapy days. Piles and piles of powder paints, papers, workbooks and guidebooks, felt tip pens, huge pots of paintbrushes, reams of cane, lino-cutting tools, and other dried out, dust-encrusted items. On one side of the room, stacked haphazardly from floor to ceiling were makeshift portfolios filled with children's drawings, each picture dated and labelled in her spidery semi-legible handwriting. Alongside them were albums of photos of the same works, also labelled and dated, bursting at the seams. She was carrying out a decades-long study, building up her evidence, complemented by her reading and illegible writing. Every wall, table, chair, surface of the house was filled with papers and books on child psychology, psychotherapy and art. She was a teacher, a student, a researcher, living and breathing her profession. It was painful to dispose of it all, but it made me remember what an incredible labour of love working with children was for her and is for many of us in the profession.

As both a parent and teacher myself, I have come to realise that one gives so much of oneself but that this giving is often done out of necessity and not always from choice. As both a parent and teacher, you can be driven to give above and beyond because you are passionately trying to do the right thing. Similarly, you can be pushed to even going against what your principled mind truly believes in because you are at the edge of your capacity to cope as a person. My mum, as a parent and as a teacher was often so unable to help others on so many occasions, including her own children, because she was so helpless herself. She was operating at the edge of and beyond her capacity so much of the time. And yet, as a teacher and as a parent, I know that she was so committed and fighting to stay committed all along. She loved the children she worked with and she loved her own children – despite the inherited demons that led her to commit crimes against them. In my own way, I think becoming a teacher was a way of continuing this legacy, but in a way that was my own.

In 2015, I left The Key and then spent three years as Head of Membership at Challenge Partners. I am now Director of Engagement for the Finnish education organisation, Lyfta. In my spare time, I am Chair of Governors at a primary school in Tottenham, on the Trust Board for the Inspire Partnership in Greenwich, a steering group member for the BAMEed Network and on the advisory board for the Teacher Toolkit. I may have left the traditional classroom environment, but I will always be a teacher, and I will always want to spend my time serving the children and adults in this wonderful, heart-filling and at times heart-wrenching sector.

Joe Gibbs

I'm in my forties and I've been married to Pete for over twenty-three years and we have two amazing sons: Fred, 20 and Albert, 16. Until January 2017, we all lived in Iver – a little village in South Bucks, I was a Lead Teacher of English at a large, mixed comprehensive in west London and I loved my job.

My husband works for Mars and after twenty-five years in the business, mainly as a Cocoa Technologist, (which has to be the coolest job ever) he was asked to move to Chicago to be a product developer for Skittles, (an even cooler job!) so we packed up and moved to the Windy City. Our eldest boy is at Bournemouth University and flies out to be with us during the holidays and our youngest boy is loving high school and life in the USA.

It's taken me a while to get used to being a 'trailing spouse' and I spent the first year mourning the loss of my job, missing my eldest son and blogging about the massive adjustment, which I am hoping to turn into a book. I had to jump through a million hoops to get my educator's licence but chose not to return to full-time teaching. I was, however, desperate to get back into the classroom, so since January 2019, I've been a substitute teacher at the two local high schools. This has been a real eyeopener: humbling and fascinating in equal measure.

But I haven't always been a teacher. In fact, it was only when researching how to get into teaching for my young cousin, that I had an epiphany and I realised that I was then one who should be a teacher. It was a thunderbolt moment.

From university, I went into publishing where I became an editorial assistant – or general dogsbody. The boss was a bully and he sacked me after six months for having what he said was 'a butterfly mind.' That knocked me for a bit, but it's that same butterfly mind that allows me to flit adeptly from project to project, to adapt and change – important qualities for a teacher.

After that rather bruising start to my career, I worked for The Duke of Edinburgh's Award at their HQ in Windsor. For five wonderful years I worked in the communications department and I was trained in desktop publishing, copywriting and editing. The charity produced all its publications in-house, including the Award's national magazine. This fostered a love of writing that later became a huge part of my teaching practice – I began a blog for my students and always loved doing the narrative/descriptive writing exam questions with them.

My students loved hearing about the many wonderful days I spent at St James's Palace and Buckingham Palace where the Gold Award ceremonies were held. It was there that I saw the difference that extracurricular activities made for the kids that gained their Award – not everything is about exam results and this was a message I consistently shared with my students, much to their surprise.

At each award ceremony, I ran the press office with my boss. We would photograph and interview all the celebrity presenters, from soap stars to scientists, footballers to explorers – each one had an inspirational story to share about their success that inspired us and the Award recipients. I danced with Sir Bruce Forsythe in St James's Palace and once had a wee on the Queen's loo, I even had a hat allowance! How all this shaped me as an educator is anyone's guess – but it makes a great anecdote!

Then came the birth of my first son and I spent a couple of years in a fog of hormones trying to be a freelance writer – mainly corporate stuff and a couple of magazines. One day, after a particularly gripping episode of *Spooks* on TV, I saw a recruitment advert in the paper for MI5. On a bit of a whim, I applied. I was basically at that stage of motherhood when I thought my brain had dissolved and I was losing all hope of ever having a 'proper career'. The advert promised flexible working and term-time only hours, which was obviously an attractive option – though sadly, almost no salary.

To my surprise, I passed the first stage interview, then a second. Before I knew it, I was at MI5 headquarters sitting a bunch of exams and quietly wondering what I'd got myself into. No one was more surprised than me when I passed the exams and was invited to a final interview where I was offered a job.

In the interests of honesty, I feel it's only fair to explain that the job wasn't anything really glamorous – it wasn't 'trainee spy' or anything, but it did require a whole fake job cover story and complete secrecy. But then, just as I was about to sign on the dotted line, I was told that there were no positions available with flexible/term-time only hours … so that was the end of that. It would have cost me more in the commute and childcare than I would have earned, but it was fun while it lasted. I always loved telling my students that I'd been recruited by MI5 – until it backfired at my last job and they totally believed I was a spy!

It was as I was working for my church as a children and families pastor, running all the children's programmes and activities and working with local schools, that I had my epiphany, did my PGCE and went into teaching. I believe that every job, every experience, led me to that decision and I like to think that my journey also helped to show my students how a degree in English can be used in a range of different jobs.

One of the parts of my job that I love the most is reading aloud to my students. When I was little, my grandfather used to listen to me read. When I was around six, he made a tape recording of me reading aloud and on it you can hear him encouraging me to use expression. I remembered this fondly while reading the final chapter of *The Woman in Black* on World Book Day, whilst dressed as The Woman in Black. This will always be a particular highlight. I am a performer at heart. I've been a member of my local amateur dramatic group since I was twelve and have acted in, written and directed many shows over the years, including performing at the Edinburgh Fringe Festival in a production of *Godspell*, where I played a prostitute! I was also a singer in a covers band for many years. I know this has shaped my teaching style. I know how to use my voice and my presence; as a little person, I have to be able to walk into a room and own it, especially on a windy Friday afternoon with Year 10!

Moving to another country and knowing no one has given me a whole new perspective on teaching. I've been given a glimpse of what it's like to be the new girl on a whole other level. Despite speaking the same language, there have been many times when I haven't been understood and this has given me greater empathy for EAL students. Taking a huge professional step back has been pretty humbling, but it's made be really evaluate what I love and don't love about teaching, it's helped me to understand what truly motivates and moves me and I'll certainly be bringing this back with me when I return to the UK.

For several years in a row, I was the proud winner of the 'Best Second Mum' Award at the Year 11 prom, so I guess that paints a bit of a picture about the kind of teacher I am. My heart is for teenagers. I love the loud ones and the quiet ones, the well-behaved ones and the naughty ones. I encourage them to give me their best and in return, I always try to give them mine. I want to walk beside them each day and tell them that I'm proud of them, whatever their academic ability. I tell them I love them and that their results are not the sum of who they are.

I'm the kind of teacher who wants to make an impact and wants the subject I teach to make an impact – I once took a horse to school when I was teaching *Equus* because most of my sixth formers had never seen a bloody horse! Of course, in hindsight, the more sensible thing would have been to take the students to the local stables ... but where's the fun in that?

I love learning. I say I'm sorry when I'm wrong. I model the behaviour I want to see. Those three things make up my ideology.

Helena Jockel
as told by her granddaughter, Dr Yolana Wassersug

Helena Jockel, my grandmother, was born in Mukačevo, part of present-day Ukraine. Before the war, it was home to a thriving Jewish community and her parents owned a bakery. Her father was stern and quite religious, while her mother was gentler and more progressive. She had seven siblings. Only three of them survived the Holocaust.

She enjoyed learning and reading, and she had a special knack for languages. Her brother, Chaim, was particularly encouraging of her educational pursuits, despite the prescribed gender roles of the time. She wrote in her autobiography that she was a high achiever, like all of her siblings and that she loved learning and enjoyed going to school. In 1940 she was admitted to a teacher training institution in Miskolc, Hungary and she received her certification in 1943. After this she was employed at a Jewish elementary school in Užhorod.

In 1944, German troops invaded Užhorod. On March 18th, all the Jews in the town were rounded up and moved into an unsanitary, overcrowded and miserable ghetto. Helena stayed with her students in the ghetto and attempted to give them comfort and care. She always described them as "her children" and tried to take solace in the fact that they were together.

A few weeks later, Helena, her children and the rest of the Jews in the ghetto, were forced into cattle cars and transported to Auschwitz. Helena saw the last glimpse of her students, as they were led away to the gas chambers. All of them were murdered. This, without a doubt, influenced her. But I can't begin to put into words how.

When she arrived at Auschwitz, after a hellish four-day journey, she exited the train and had the awful thought that this was where she was going to die. She was assigned to Auschwitz-Birkenau to be an able-bodied worker.

She spoke about the lack of privacy – they were constantly watched by guards with guns, whose cruelty knew no bounds. She learnt that every few months, the workers changed. They fantasised that this meant that they had escaped but the thick black smoke and smell of burning human flesh told a different story. The conditions were horrendous, with mud floors, pallets for beds and a leaking roof. Holes in the floor served as toilets and insects and rats were everywhere. People died of disease due to these unsanitary conditions, but none of this compared to the constant fear of being taken away: they could kill two thousand people in two hours.

When she arrived at Auschwitz, she made friends with a Polish girl called Regina who managed to get her work in the kitchens, where she could attempt to keep clean and sneak a little bit more food for her and her friends. Even though the days were gruelling, with back-breaking work, she managed to find some camaraderie with the other women working there. When the guards weren't around, they would take comfort from singing Hebrew songs; somehow this gave them encouragement and lifted their spirits, taking their thoughts away from death and killing for a short time.

Amazingly, all of the terrible things she experienced during the war, including the deaths of her young pupils, did not crush her passion for teaching. As soon as it was possible for her to teach again after the war ended, she found a way to get back into the job. She passed exams to re-certify as a teacher. Post-war, she had a renewed desire to educate children about the values of the world.

After the war, she made the switch from teaching elementary school children to high school students and taught languages and literature, Russian literature in particular. This change was for practical reasons: there was a shortage of high school teachers in post-war Czechoslovakia. Getting a job, and getting one quickly, allowed her to re-gain control over her life and have stability. The job made it possible for her to have a sense of normalcy in her family life and raise her children: this was an important part of her healing.

It's really hard to identify an ethos or ideology that guided her teaching. I doubt that she would have thought of her work in those terms. She was a practical and pragmatic person, who recognised that teaching was the right type of job for her. Quite simply, it was her job, and she was good at it. Having said that, she had a reputation for relating to students on a personal level and forming friendships with students. She was good at learning and remembering every student's name ... even decades later, she'd still remember them! Many of her students kept in touch with her long after they had graduated. She loved teaching and enjoyed contributing positively to students' lives.

One important thing to note is that she was passionate about teaching, but she was not always willing to teach about the Holocaust. In fact, in the aftermath of the war, she rarely spoke about the terrible things she experienced. She did not tell her students about what happened to her in detail, although they did know that she had survived the camps. Helena couldn't talk about this time in her life with her family either – including with her children, Pavel and Jana. She was very reluctant to educate others about the war. This is partially due to the fact that she was living in a communist country where she didn't have the same right to free speech that you or I enjoy. However, even if she had been allowed to speak freely, she probably stayed quiet on the subject because of post-traumatic stress.

Much later in her life, she experienced an important change that made it possible for her to speak and to finally educate others about the Holocaust. This change occurred after she retired and emigrated to Canada in 1988, at the age of 69. Her two children (Jana and Pavel) and her three grandchildren (Tom, Dan, and Yolana) were all living in Canada already. Even though her professional career as a teacher was over, she took on a new role of being an educator and caretaker for her grandchildren, caring for them from eight o'clock in the morning until her daughter finished work in the evening. She enjoyed walking her granddaughter to and from primary school and reading lots of stories together. In this new phase of her life, Helena finally had the freedom to start talking about the holocaust in a direct way. She was finally emotionally ready to talk about the war, and she was finally in a country where it was safe to do so: Helena brought her skill as an educator out of her workplace and into her family.

My grandmother became a Holocaust educator late in her life. Her youngest grandchild (me) was a teenager, and no longer needed a babysitter. She felt that this was her chance to make a contribution in another way and she began to speak frequently about the Holocaust to anyone who would listen. She gave talks about her experiences at church meeting halls, book clubs, public libraries, and university classrooms. In this phase of her life, she was finally able to organise her thoughts about the Holocaust into her autobiography – *We Sang in Hushed Voices*. She felt she needed to write the book and to educate others, despite the fact that it was painful and traumatic. She began to see that, as a survivor, she had an obligation to bear witness.

The educational work she did when she was a Russian literature teacher in Czechoslovakia was characterised by a passion for the subject, a love of her students, and a desire to have a fulfilling career. In contrast, the educational work she did when she was a senior citizen and a Holocaust educator in Canada was characterised by a sense of duty, and a desire to provide testimony of the Holocaust. She believed that sharing her trauma could help students be vigilant in the fight against intolerance and hatred. These two modes of teaching represent two different phases of her life, and two very different experiences for her. But she was deeply committed to both.

Caroline Riggs

I have been teaching Secondary Science for over eleven years, but originally, I studied for a degree in 'Human Psychology with Professional Training.' As part of the course, I worked in a Neurological Rehabilitation Centre as an Assistant Psychologist, working with patients who had suffered brain injury.

As part of my work on my assistant psychologist placement, I helped deliver a program that taught the patients and their families about the structure of the brain, so that they could understand their treatment better. I loved the teaching element to the job, so I made the decision to apply for a PGCE in biology.

After I completed my PGCE, I started working at a secondary school in Worthing and during my second year, I signed up for a PGCE in physics (due to a shortage of physics specialists in my school), spending one day a week at university retraining. The course was great – it was a lot of work, but the course tutors really understood the pressures of teaching. As with my PGCE, the most valuable support came from my colleagues on the course: a solidarity with a tough workload! We helped each other out with the work and the infectious enthusiasm made it easier to balance. In science it is fairly common for someone to have done a subject knowledge enhancement course (usually in physics or chemistry, as these are supported by government funding), so there were plenty of people like me on the course.

After six years, I moved schools to a role as Head of Psychology and spent four years teaching Science to 11 to 18-year-olds, including psychology and physics A-levels. This was an exciting and busy time, as I was also leading the Extended Project Qualification (EPQ). This school had great facilities for special educational needs, so I was able to take basic training in Braille and British Sign Language to support my pupils with significant sensory impairments. This experience made me improve my explanations for every pupil. For example, when I talked about the National Grid, I was assuming that the whole class knew what a pylon was – and most did, but for a pupil who was partially sighted and therefore hadn't seen them out of the car windows like the other pupils, I needed to be clearer when I talked. I learnt to describe more, to make offhanded definitions in the middle of my sentences, or to use a variety of pictures or words to explain the same thing. Now I plan my lessons by spending time thinking through what someone would have to already know to access what I'm about to talk about – right down to "did they hear about that earthquake last week on the radio?"

Since my NQT year, I have worked with several organisations that provide science outreach and science communication events to schools and members of the public. Through this work, I have given talks, run family events, written scripts for educational videos and most recently written a book with a colleague (*The Little book of Psychology* – Caroline Riggs and Emily Ralls). This year I have moved schools to a role where I can teach 11 to 16-year-olds, as well as developing further science communication projects with companies like Incredible Oceans and Brighton Science Festival.

Although I started out as an Assistant Psychologist, I feel like even the part-time jobs I did while I was at university have shaped me into the teacher I am today. My AP placement was my first introduction to teaching and it helped me to plan based on the needs of the individuals I was in front of. It also made me consider why I was teaching the content I was – how is it going to improve somebody's life?

Throughout university, I had part-time jobs to support my study; these ranged from working in the Sea Life Centre, to bar work and shop work. I feel like all of these jobs helped me to learn how to interact with people, manage my time and learn from people with different talents and aspirations. The best team I worked with was the management team at a restaurant; they made the place feel like a caring supportive family – something that is vital in teaching, for wellbeing!

The science communication work I do allows me to come into contact with scientists from many different areas. It really helps me to stay on top of developments so that I can use great stories and examples in my classroom teaching. I love listening to the different ways that people explain their work, and it has helped me become a good presenter and to explain complicated information in an engaging way – even to people with no science experience, or loads!

For example, through my work with Incredible Oceans I have been able to develop activities for physics lessons that use the context of the ocean. When we talk about pressure, we look at the adaptations creatures have made to survive deep in the sea; when we look at how sound waves travel we look at how the sperm whale is the loudest sound on earth and could communicate across the world!

Through my school I have also started working with a charity who set up a school for children living in a poor area, just outside Mombasa. I have made several trips out there (three with some of my pupils), to work with their teachers and students in very different facilities than the ones in the UK. From a classroom point of view, it improved my own teaching, as during my NQT year I was very reliant on technology and I suddenly had no electricity or resources in a classroom. I had to plan and think carefully about how I was going to explain. I worked through a slight loss of confidence and ultimately, I feel I am a better teacher for it.

The pupils that we took out to work in the school with us were incredible. Initially I was worried about how they would react emotionally to being confronted with the poverty that their peers in this part of the world experienced. But their actions and attitudes were truly inspirational. Some students took up paper rounds on their return to pay for school supply donations and many continued to fundraise for the charity long after they left education themselves. At the school there was some "interesting" wildlife ... on seeing a large spider in one of the classrooms, I once told a pupil that I was scared of them. I asked the pupil what they were scared of and they replied, "losing my education." This stuck with me and I try to remember each day that whilst it may appear to us that some of our students don't value their time at school, it is up to us to teach them this and to give them as many opportunities as we can to see how valuable and precious their education is.

When we were there, we arrived at 9 a.m. and left at 4 p.m., but the teaching day was much longer than this, with some pupils studying for as long as the sun was up. The school has grown into some bigger buildings over the years, through the charity's hard work. But the first few years, we took our pupils to visit there and some classes were cramped into small spaces around a blackboard, using pencils in exercise books, so that they could turn back to the start, erase and use the book again when they got to the end. Despite this, the pupils are so dedicated to their studies, and the staff there are amazing at teaching them.

We had an interesting inset day session, where we shared the best parts of our teaching. The Kenyan teachers taught me how to question better – all pupils in their classroom are expected to answer, anyone could be asked and saying "I don't know" didn't get you out of it! They were interested in our classroom displays and how we had examples of pupil work up. Also, that we share learning objectives with the pupils, so they know what to expect from a lesson. It was clear from both schools that the most precious thing was that all staff knew their students well and made the best decisions for their situations and personalities. That one inset day has continued to inspire me for years and years afterwards. I always try to think about what the impact of any school policy or lesson approach will be on the pupils. Which sounds obvious but it is easy to forget.

As a science teacher, I firmly believe that pupils should always work things out for themselves. Instead of teaching them some facts, I love the lessons where they can experiment and find their own conclusions. I try to include a context for every lesson – a book they could read, a career they could go into, or a story about how this particular science is used in the world and their everyday life. I strongly believe that we should always talk about the WHY of each lesson. Even though the question, "but Miss, why are we bothering to learn this? When will we ever use it?" is really annoying, it is very important that we know the answer!

The best thing about my subject is that it is changing. The fact that I am teaching different facts and telling different stories compared to when I first started, shows just how much science has moved on in recent years. I really do love my job. I love that you never have the same lesson twice and it is rewarding to see pupils work out science concepts for themselves.

Rachael Maddocks

I was brought up in the Northern town of St Helens, near Liverpool, which has a reputation of being quite a grim, deprived area. Growing up, I felt like I didn't fit in and had quite a rough time, as I was different from those around me. When you stand out as a teenager, that unfortunately makes you a target for unkind behaviour. I hated school but loved the lessons and from about age thirteen, I started to really get into my English and media lessons and decided that I wanted to become a journalist. I had a real passion for writing and started writing for local papers and magazines. I then went on to study a joint Honours English and Media degree at Salford University.

I went to Salford at a really exciting time. The BBC and ITV were just relocating there from London and there was a real buzz about the place. But, my limited experience of journalism had made me realise that it was a tough job – where you had to be willing to do anything in pursuit of a story, including compromise your morals and sell people out. I didn't want to do this. I also had a burning desire to change people's lives and make a difference: cliché I know, but true! I wanted to be that teacher who kids remembered and left saying, "she never gave up on me."

I didn't go into teaching straight away. I worked at Apple all the way through university and continued this for a year after graduating. This job taught me so much about being patient and building effective relationships. As a company, Apple are really excellent at placing the emphasis on people and without even realising it at the time, this definitely shaped me into the teacher I would become. I am often praised still for my patience with the children and this definitely came from my experiences there. I think this is something which is sometimes missing in schools – teachers no longer seem to be at the centre of what schools are doing. The human aspect has sometimes been taken out of the classroom but if teachers build the relationships, the results will then come.

When I was considering applying for a teacher training place, I remembered what it was like for me at school. I ended up moving schools in Year 10 and the new school I moved to was doing a completely different exam board from my former school, so I had to cram two years' worth of work into one. It just showed how determined I was, so I applied for a PGCE place and started my teaching journey.

Along with my goal of making a difference, I wanted to make sure that I didn't waste my degree. It is hard when you do a subject like English as it can be difficult to find a career where you can utilise it properly. A lot of people end up in jobs which are not related to their specialism and I was determined not to do that! However, I did know I didn't want to teach primary. My mum was a primary school teacher and I knew I didn't possess the patience; I wanted to work with disaffected teenagers, which is quite funny, as these are the pupils, I have the most difficulties with now!

After a few years in a secondary school, I made the move to teach in a further education college in a large, deprived town in the North West. I teach English Language GCSE resits, so many of the pupils I teach can be quite switched off about school. My entire job is trying to get kids that golden Grade 4, which they have to have to move on to apprenticeships, employment or further study. It can be like pulling teeth sometimes, but I have to remember that many of these pupils hated school and their English lessons and really don't want to be in the position they are – resitting English.

But at times, it is also the most rewarding job in the world. In my first year at the college, I started in the February, so I really didn't have much time to push my classes to where I wanted them to be. But come results day, I was thrilled to see that one child got a Grade 5. I know to some teachers, this is still a low grade, but this boy had come to the college with a Grade 3, so his progress was immense. He was dedicated and came to the extra sessions and put in the work, including trying his best in class. But he did have very low self-confidence and I see part of my job as being able to boost his confidence. But isn't that the nature of our jobs? Very often, kids see us as teacher-robots, but there is so much more to our jobs than just teaching them to pass exams. He said to me on results day, "Nobody has ever taken the time to get to know me and understand me." All of that just because I spent a bit of time with him.

I did think when I started the resit role, that I would struggle to build relationships with the pupils in the way that you do at secondary schools. I teach a lot of the pupils for one year, although I do have some returning students. I don't see them as often as my students in Year 10 and 11 when I worked in secondary education, but in some ways, I feel that you are able to build stronger relationships with college kids. There seems to be less of a barrier there. They don't call me "Miss" – I am "Rachel," and this fosters a more mature and adult relationship, where we can truly teach them like the young adults they are. A lot of the students long for this in Year 11 but they are restricted by too many rules, such as uniforms and the environment with all of its responsibilities and pressure. It is a different kind of culture in a college and I definitely prefer it.

My endometriosis diagnosis was part of the reason that I stopped teaching in secondary schools. I knew that I wouldn't be able to keep up the pace and the long hours, bringing stacks of books home to mark of an evening. The stress and the pressure of working in a secondary school is constant and I knew that my body would just not be able to cope with it anymore.

I am very honest with the students I teach, and I tell them that I am dealing with a chronic illness every day when I come to work. They know that sometimes I won't be in college as I am in so much pain that I cannot physically get out of bed. I have explained what endometriosis is to them: that I have non-cancerous tumours all over my body and they grow and stuck all of my organs together. Many of them have parents or relatives that have chronic illnesses and that definitely helps them relate a bit more to me. They see me as a human and have a certain level of understanding, so when I am not in, they just accept it. When I am there, they appreciate it more and know that I am teaching these high-quality lessons despite being in a lot of pain.

It has got to the point now, that despite several bouts of surgery, I am in an excruciating amount of pain often and some amount of pain every day. During my most recent surgery in July, I was also diagnosed with adenomyosis, where the lining of my uterus is breaking up through the muscles and into the nerves, causing a lot of pain. In addition to this, I have a lot of adhesions and scar tissue from previous surgeries which also cause me pain, so I am really struggling. I have to take a lot of medication to get through the day.

On top of all of this, my conditions have affected my bladder and bowels, which can give me seconds notice that I need to use the bathroom – not great for a teacher! I do wonder, if I had continued to teach in a traditional school setting, whether I would still be able to do my job? Probably not.

Aside from copious amounts of Codeine, I get through each day with the motivating thought that I am creating a good life for my son, so that really helps mentally. If I am really struggling, I just try to break it down and take one day at a time – sometimes even an hour at a time if need be. I also get a huge amount of help from support groups because I get to talk to lots of other women who also suffer like I do.

Of course, the support of my husband also helps and when I am not spending time with him and my son, I love to read and have days out with family. This helps me get through the bad days.

My ethos is that I want my students to have the kind of experience I didn't at school. I don't want to see them as a number. Some of the kids I teach have been labelled as 'challenging' because they struggled academically, and teachers would have done anything to get them out of the classroom. I want to show them they are more than a grade, but obviously, sometimes I get it wrong. Occasionally, I will meet a child that I just cannot reach as hard as I try. But I do have boundaries... I might be friendly, but I am not their friend. I am there to teach them and ensure that they have the confidence to achieve everything that they need to.

Christine Owen

Over twenty years ago, I changed my life after leaving London and the madness of the music industry. Teaching, I thought, would give me an academic and personal challenge and fit into my new life as a mother. I thought it was time to grow up. My sister had already retrained as a primary teacher, after working as a manager in industry.

I was never the studious, compliant student at school. I daydreamed. Nobody expected me to achieve very much because I didn't put much effort into things that I had no interest in. I was only interested in music. But I managed to be a female in a male-centred industry, which is not that common. My school happily ejected me at age sixteen and suggested that I didn't have the academic ability for A-levels. They had previously told my sister that she was too intelligent to be a teacher! Careers advice wasn't up to much in those days. But I decided to give it a go anyway.

I have now been a teacher for about twenty years, including roles as a Head of Year 10/11, Head of House, Literacy Co-ordinator and now a Head of English.

In my previous life, I was a music journalist. I started out by interviewing goth bands in the mid-1980s, knocking on backstage doors, meeting my black and bleached-haired heroes and making my own fanzine. I would type it, print it, letterset the headlines and then sell them at gigs.

Later, at university, I became Music Editor of the university newspaper for three years, right at the start of the exciting Britpop era. Every evening was spent at Rock City in Nottingham, Derby Warehouse or Leicester Princess Charlotte, interviewing such legendary bands as Oasis, Gene, Sleeper, Cast, The Bluetones and sharing their riders backstage. This led to some unlikely experiences, such as playing Jenga at the Holiday Inn reception with Oasis and the band Squeeze; sitting in a box next to Liam Gallagher at the Albert Hall who, potentially, hadn't lost his voice when he said he had, leaving Noel to sing the whole set; hanging out with The La's in Liverpool backstage, when they had turned up worse for wear, thinking they were supporting the band – when that date was later that month in Brighton; most of the time, blagging a space in hotel rooms because we couldn't afford a hotel room ourselves. But undoubtedly, one of the best things was to have backstage access at music festivals because of the access to flushing, sanitary toilets.

I then moved to London and worked at *Vox*, a national music paper for a while. I was right in the middle of a very exciting time in music, living my dream in Camden Town, interviewing musicians and then working in punk PR with more bands including The Offspring, Rancid, NOFX and The Vandals among others.

In Brighton, when working at *Vox*, I found myself having to blast out of the back doors of a venue with the band and being shoved into the back of a tour van while screaming fans were trying to get their hands on the van; I feel I experienced vicariously what it was like to be a rock 'n' roll star! At this point, I was also commissioned to write a couple of books – one on Beck and another on the Charlatans. The former wasn't published in my name because of a change of publishers and the latter only published in Chinese! Therefore, neither book has my name on, which is most irritating!

Going to gigs was fun, but I needed to pay my bills. A moment of serendipity led me to working at the officers of the managers of the some of the most prolific and respected musicians in rock 'n' roll history; bands such as The Who, Jimmy Page, and Robert Plant and Judas Priest. Before long, I was chatting happily to Pete Townshend, having my shoulders massaged by Robert Plant and working on organising the Quadrophenia tour, which had a host of famous names working on it including Phil Daniels and Billy Idol. Most strangely, weekly telephone calls came in from Reggie Kray, who would call from prison to speak to my boss who was not often in. The first time he called, I thought someone was having a laugh, but after a few days, nothing was surprising.

After this, I moved to MTV in Camden and worked as a talent escort – finding myself at the EMA Awards, looking after the Spice Girls for the weekend and leaning over the balcony watching them cavort with Robbie Williams. These experiences gave me great confidence; having tackled Liam Gallagher more than once in interviews, working for a steely East End friend of the Krays and learning how to deal with some very tricky well-known celebrities, dealing with students was something which seemed very familiar to me!

Due to my winding path to teaching, I want others to find their own way into their chosen careers too, even if they don't know what it actually is they want to achieve yet. I get students who are not driven, and I bring this attitude into my lessons. I use my sense of humour, attempting to make those students who think that they aren't bright or who disappear in a classroom feel valued – and feel like they can. I am glad I took a circuitous route to teaching. I certainly wasn't grown up until I had a child of my own – and I now bring an empathy and wry take on life which the students seem to respect.

Earlier, I talked about needing to grow up, which almost makes teaching seem boring but it's definitely not! For me, the best part is the students. I am never bored by spending so much of my time with them – and they never fail to surprise me, make me laugh, make me feel such pride. They challenge me in so many ways: with my desire to hook them, with their really pertinent questions and sometimes when I need to help with personal problems. Of course, I get the best tips on a wild array of things: music I should listen to; a book I should read; their new words they enlighten me about – which they find most amusing when I use! I feel I am in touch with the world far more through all of the issues, YouTubers, influencers, and computer games that they talk about and use in their own writing. It keeps you current. I can't imagine working with just adults like I used to. As a teacher, I find it so rewarding to help them along the way during their formative years to be the very best they can be and this is much more exciting than journalism.

Having said that, I am a no-nonsense teacher. I expect respect. I'm intuitive enough to know that everybody has their off days and I know when to push and challenge (which is most of the time) but I also know when to pull back and give space. I like to make every student realises that they have the capacity to succeed – I love to introduce them to the sometimes poignant, surprising and shocking nature of books and their messages. It really is a joy when a student can identify with the characters or learn from the story. Holden

Caulfield in *Catcher in the Rye* has enabled students to realise feeling angst and suffering from loss is hard, but that they aren't alone with those feelings. Or when you detect supressed tears when a student realises Scout never saw Arthur 'Boo' Radley again, after the timid man cared so much as to venture out and save them. It really is heart-warming.

I am not sure the current novellas I teach have touched students as much emotionally – with the new focus on pre-19th century texts. The old male characters of Scrooge or Henry Jekyll can certainly teach us something – but do they connect in the same way? Probably not. I want students to be curious and to embrace words, because with a world of words, they can articulate themselves and precisely explain themselves. This is not only good for their writing, or their business meetings, but words—along with reading fiction—are crucial to well-being.

Sue Rogers

When I was at school, all I ever wanted to be was a hairdresser. I spent most of my last two years of school skipping lessons – I was too interested in boys and having fun. I didn't have particularly academic aspirations; I needed three grade Cs to get on to my hairdressing course, so that's what I aimed for. I didn't really try as I felt that I didn't really need to. I figured that even if I didn't get the results, I could still go into hairdressing, but it would just take me a bit longer, as I would start at a lower level. Luckily, I got the results I needed and spent eighteen months at college, learning how to be a hairdresser. After this, I spent several years working in a salon and then in 1998 I set up my own business as a mobile hairdresser.

I had never even considered becoming a teacher. I fell into teaching as I signed up for an evening course to learn how to do make-up. Increasingly, I was finding that I was getting a lot of wedding clients, so I thought that by also learning how to do make-up, I could increase my business by doing bridal packages. It wasn't anything fancy, just basic wedding make-up but there were a couple of women on my course, whose second language was English, and they were struggling. So, I started to help them with their assignments and some of the terminology the tutor was using that they didn't understand. The tutor pulled me to the side and asked me if I had ever thought of teaching, as she thought I would be really good at it.

At first, I didn't really give it a second thought, but there was a recession on the horizon and as somebody who was self-employed, if a client cancelled, it meant that I would be unable to pay bills. Therefore, financially it made sense ... so I did my teaching course and qualified. Once I was actually in the classroom, I realised what a brilliant decision I had made as I absolutely loved it. What's more, I was good at it! As I am teaching Level 1 hairdressers, who have failed their English and maths at GCSE, I can relate to them, as I am from a humble background, I am not an academic person who excelled at school myself. I could give the message to my students, that you don't have to be a grade A student to get to where you want to be and be successful.

A lot of the students I teach already feel like a failure by the time they get to us. They already haven't managed to achieve the grades that the government wanted them to achieve in English and maths. It really upsets me that by not achieving a grade 4, these pupils think they have failed – they haven't. They just didn't get the government's notion of a pass. They have such low self-esteem as they feel already branded as a failure at only sixteen years old. Some of them have been disengaged from school for a long time, often sitting in lessons doing nothing because they were unable to access the work. Others just stopped turning up. I like to think I am setting them on that stepping stone, down the path of where they want to be.

Around four years ago, we set up a hairdressing management degree course at the college I work at, so that now, students have the chance to graduate with a BA (Honours) degree. So, we have just had students who have started out on a Level 1 course with me and have now come out with a degree. Amazing!

I remember, in the first year of my teaching career, there was a girl who had been kicked out of school and she had been completely written off. But every year, we have a 'Student of the Year' award and my first nomination was this girl. This pretty much sums up my educational ethos: to support the underdog, who everybody else has given up on. It was this ethos which led to me setting up my alternative modelling agency, 'Rogue Model Management.'

It all started when I was thirty-nine – I had never modelled before, but I had always wanted to do a photoshoot and a photographer in Bolton was offering a makeover and shoot for a crazy low price, as somebody had cancelled. So, I went and had the shoot and it was a great experience and with this newfound confidence, I applied for a modelling competition online, with a clothing company, to become a sponsored model with their company. I was astounded to come second, and it made me think – I can do this! But juggling alternative modelling with education is tough and despite never having done anything that could be construed as risqué, my boss at the time was not happy with what I was doing, so I decided to put this on the backburner and plough my efforts into supporting other models – and this is where the modelling agency was born.

Originally, we had no intention of Rogue being as big as it has become. It started out as a modelling group where we were helping girls who were having trouble getting themselves noticed, but then we started to get bookings and ended up running our own events. Now we have over 100 models on our books, from all corners of the UK and we've had some of our models in horror movies, in shoots for clothing companies and performing at events.

The models we sign are not your conventional models. They come in all shapes and sizes – from a size 8 to a size 22. Some of them have brightly coloured hair, piercings and tattoos. You wouldn't really see them on the cover of *Vogue*. But people want models that are different and unconventional. These days you see a lot of alternative looking people who never would have thought that they could become a model, but they can. Anyone can do anything they can put their mind to.

The agency work has led to me taking on the running of the English chapter of 'Pin Ups against Bullying' which is an organisation where models provide support to those who may be being bullied. This is a cause which is close to my heart as I was bullied at school for being alternative and then my daughter was also bullied. I just wanted to provide an ear for people, even it was just for them to have a little rant and for me to agree with them, that what was happening to them wasn't acceptable. This is something I also strongly advocate in college too. Some of the kids come and they have even been bullied by staff and told that they were "thick" as they didn't get things their teacher taught them at GCSE level. The world would be a lot better if we were all a bit kinder and thought about the gravity of our words.

Kate McAllister

I was born in East London in the early 70s and raised in Essex. I left school with two GCSEs, an A in French and a B in art. School wasn't a place where I felt especially welcome or valued and no one ever expected me to amount to much, so I don't think anyone was surprised. On #worldteacherday I sat for a long time trying to think of a single teacher who influenced me when I was young, but I couldn't come up with a single shareable memory from my own school career.

I felt different at school, like I didn't fit in. It started in infant school and by the time I reached secondary, my self-image as a learner was painfully low. I wasn't actively difficult, just disinterested; what you'd call a low-level disruptor in today's parlance. I was excluded a couple of times for minor misdemeanours. I confessed to having been involved in a water balloon battle on sports day because another girl with a similar haircut had been misidentified and was being unjustly punished. I stood up in assembly and identified myself as the culprit they sought and was swiftly suspended for my trouble. That taught me an interesting lesson about honesty being the best policy. I also got caught smoking whilst wearing school uniform and was suspended again. I don't think either misdemeanour was as life changing as having the message that I really wasn't welcome hammered home to me. As a punishment for smoking, I was cut from all the sports teams. I subsequently lost all enthusiasm for school and spent most lessons wandering in corridors. I skipped most of Year 10, which contributed to me fluffing my GCSEs. I was part of the first ever cohort of GCSEs and there was an emphasis on coursework for the first time. I didn't have much coursework completed and no one really seemed to care, so that was that. Looking back, it is clear to see how these formative experiences influenced my beliefs on inclusion and how important it is to make sure every child feels like they matter, whether they're 'good' at school learning or not.

I retook my maths and English plus a couple of other GCSEs at the local college. I achieved mediocre results, but they were enough to get me the five C grade and above passes that I needed. I then left home, moved to London and began the first of many unremarkable jobs. I had a fair few jobs before becoming a teacher. I worked as a receptionist straight out of college, which is where I taught myself to type so that I could become a secretary. I did this by reading a novel and learning to touch type as I went. When I became a secretary, I taught myself shorthand so that I could become a PA. When I became a PA, I asked if I could shadow the account managers, so that I could become a junior account manager. I was eager to learn and progress and this started a journey of self-improvement and love of learning that continues to this day.

I left London at the ripe old age of twenty to work my way around the world. The advertising industry in the early 90s wasn't a great place to be if you were a young woman in a supporting role –

#MeToo wasn't a thing back then and I'd had enough already. I took the £200 I had saved and decided I would get a job at Euro Disney which had just opened ... but I got as far as Paris, fell in love and that was the end of my travel plans. I got a job as a waitress while I taught myself to speak passable French. Once I'd learned enough French, I got a job as a secretary in an IT firm where I taught myself some rudimentary IT skills. From there I got a job as a bilingual legal secretary where I taught myself to touch type super-fast on a French keyboard and learned a LOT of legal jargon in two languages very quickly.

I got married, gave birth to my wonderful son, moved to the countryside and taught English to local teens on and off for a couple of years until I got divorced, moved back to the UK and had to seriously reconsider my life options! I needed a job that would support the two of us, enable me to spend quality time with my son and provide enough scope for future options. I'd quite enjoyed working with the teenagers in France, so teaching seemed like a very sensible option. I applied to my local university to do the BA Hons with QTS. It was a two-year course, which crammed a degree and ITT into two years. It was a truly deranged idea considering I had a three-year-old to care for however; I didn't know that at the time. It seemed like the quickest route to attaining all the things I thought I needed in life. I enrolled, took the French competency exams and waited. A short while later, I received a phone call to inform me that although I had passed the entrance tests there was the small matter of me not actually having any A-levels to address. I asked for a meeting with the course leaders and I blagged like I'd never blagged in my life before. Thankfully it worked. I got them to allow me to do the first year of an education degree as an 'access' course, despite only having a mediocre set of GCSE results to my name. I am eternally grateful to the university for giving me that chance. I do know how lucky I am to have found someone willing to invest in me at that point in my life.

I got on to the BA course the following year, having thoroughly enjoyed the education studies, and after what felt like five minutes, I graduated with QTS and started as an NQT. If you had asked me then I would have told you that my reasons for becoming a teacher were pragmatic rather than impassioned. But, with hindsight, maybe I also wanted to be the person that I needed when I was fourteen, but never met. I think that's why I gravitated to challenging schools and 'at risk' students.

Within four years, I was leading a department and had become obsessed with Learning to Learn, self-managed learning and the social and emotional aspects of learning. Making learning accessible is still what drives me nearly twenty years later. I have by no means cracked effective inclusion, but the more people I meet and the more I learn, the more possible it feels that we might collectively crack it one day.

I believe, right in my bones, that everyone can become an effective learner given the right conditions. This is what led me to co-create inclusive models such as Learning Skills, Crisis Classroom (a pop-up model for education in emergencies) and the Human Hive. They build from the bottom up as opposed to being designed from the top down. With Learning Skills, we shifted our focus from what students were learning to how they were learning it. Becoming more adept at using metacognition, self-regulation and oracy skills meant they were better able to transfer their 'learning skills' throughout the school. We could measure the program's success in improved GCSE results and the shrinking of the pupil premium gap. But what we didn't measure at the time, was the impact it had on well-being and the sense of empowerment the students felt. If I had my time again, I'd measure that too. In 2015, Dr James Mannion and I started rethinking-ed.org so that we could work with teachers who wanted to implement and evaluate similar interventions in their context. I am incredibly lucky that I now get to work with inspirational and innovative teachers all over the world. Especially given that I got a bit sidetracked along the way!

My new career as a teacher trainer happened to coincide with the arrival of thousands of refugees in Europe. Like many people, I felt I wanted to do something helpful, so I went to see if I could put my spare teacher skills to good use. What started out as a personal response quickly turned into something much bigger. It all began with a bright yellow double-decker bus that I decided to buy on eBay. My idea was met with a breathtaking outpouring of solidarity and support, and together with a bunch of amazing people, we successfully crowdfunded to buy it and turn it into a solar powered school. We took it to the Jungle refugee camp in Calais where it became a haven where people could come and learn together. I lived and worked in Calais for six months and gained a whole new perspective on what it is like to be excluded. Over the subsequent four years the idea grew far beyond the bus and developed into a whole ecosystem, called The Human Hive, which supports learning and development in a range of contexts. Darren Abrahams and I have since reached over 8,000 educators with our model and it feels like we are only just beginning. If you multiply those 8,000 educators by the number of students they will teach in their lifetime, it kind of blows my mind how far the ripples might reach.

The common thread in all this is empowerment. The Human Hive exists to make it easier for people to learn the things they want to learn, wherever they happen to be in life. I think what drives me is making models for education that aren't riddled with invisible barriers or are exclusive by design – a luxury that only certain people are afforded. I want to make it possible for people to learn what they want to learn, when they want to learn it. No matter who they are, no matter where they are, no matter what.

I am constantly being influenced by the people I meet, the things I learn and the experiences I have. In recent years I have been learning more about trauma, yoga, Ayurveda and the neurobiological, mind-body connection. What I am learning is influencing my thinking enormously. I find myself drawn to models that explain the human experience from an integrated perspective. I often think we disintegrate the learning experience in schools and focus on the mind, to the exclusion of the body, as if they were separate entities. However, the two are interconnected and one influences the other, whether we notice it or not. The more attuned we are and the safer we feel internally, the bigger our prefrontal cortex becomes and the more able we are to learn effectively. To me, it makes absolute sense to integrate mind and body and to learn how they influence each other at school. A person who can recognise and regulate their emotional state is better able to manage their own impulses and the cognitive load required for effective learning. It seems logical to me that with these skills, they will also be better able to manage life's ups and downs in adulthood.

What I have gradually come to realise is that things I was doing intuitively fifteen years ago to promote feelings of safety and belonging in my classroom and a sense of empowerment in my students, had a grounding in neuroscience – I just didn't know it then. Asking students how they were feeling while I took the register, meant that I could tell, just by the tone of voice or choice of language, who needed extra attention or how long it might take to get the class 'ready' to participate fully in the lesson. Building in time at the beginning of the lesson to notice how students were feeling and responding accordingly and leaving time at the end of the lesson to 'complete' an experience, made the whole business of learning feel safer and more enjoyable for all of us. What I didn't realise at the time was that we were learning how to co-regulate together.

My lack of confidence in my own academic abilities meant that I bumbled around figuring things out by myself for too many years. I was convinced that any day someone would discover that I didn't have any A-levels, I was clearly an idiot and didn't belong in a school, so I learned to work just under the radar. I certainly didn't have the vocabulary to talk about trauma-informed practice, metacognition or self-regulation when I first started teaching. I just had a gut feeling and my own observations and experiences to go on. I continued to teach myself as I always had; one step at a time. However, eventually I learned to take my own medicine – I guess you can't teach Learning to Learn all day every day without some of it rubbing off on you! Now I know how to learn from and alongside others too. I know now that I'm not alone and I am much braver and less inclined to make excuses for my existence or my ideas. I am fortunate to work alongside people who know much more than I do, who challenge my thinking and who are willing to share their wisdom with me. I sometimes feel like the biggest beneficiary of all my efforts to build inclusive education models has been me.

Now I get to work with educators all over the world who want to work in a more integrated and inclusive way. Sometimes they work in refugee camps, sometimes on the streets, or in homes with excluded youth. Sometimes they work in beautiful private schools with the most privileged kids on the planet. It's funny how life goes.

Vic Goddard

I was the youngest of four kids and we grew up on a council estate in South London. My sister passed her Eleven Plus exam but my two older brothers failed theirs, so they went to the local comprehensive and my sister went to the grammar. My dad was not a teacher – he was a plumber and my mum was a housewife, who had previously worked in the civil service before I was born. We were proper working class and money was tight; my dad had a white, works van and we travelled round in that – there was no car. Although they didn't work in education, they threw themselves into our school lives, by always turning up to everything. In addition, my mum was Chair of the PTA and my dad was Chair of Governors – even though he had left school at sixteen and wasn't the most literate man. I just lived school. I have childhood memories of being at all of my brother's school fêtes and education and the role of the school was just a massive part of our lives. My older brother went on to become a teacher, then my second brother and then my sister... I was determined not to be a teacher and then I realised that was what I really wanted to do! It just seemed like a natural thing to do.

During my own school years, I had a great experience. I went to an all-boys school in South London and I was clever and sporty and if you are sporty in a boys' school, you get massive brownie points. I speak to others sometimes who I went to school with who tell me about the negative experiences they had but my time there just wasn't like that. I had great parents, who were involved and interested and a school who really nurtured me. There was a Headteacher there, who had been at the school for a long time and his name was Ernie Kingsbury. I remember he used to refer to the school as a 'family unit' and I remember smirking at the time and thinking 'what an old fart he is!' But now I hear myself saying that all the time! One of the phrases which is similar to this and I use all the time is 'family comes in many forms' because this is our family when we are at work and we have to look after each other. I try to pretend that this isn't influenced by Ernie Kingsbury, when I was eleven years old, but it probably is. I feel very fortunate for the support I had at school and from my parents and I look at some of the lads I grew up with at school and they weren't given the opportunities I was.

I started out as a PE teacher and did that for ten years before I moved on to start various positions on the Senior Leadership Team. I loved being a PE teacher and felt like they were paying me for my hobby, which was just phenomenal. But I had pretty much always wanted to be a Head and I remember the exact moment I knew I wanted it: I was fourteen. At the time, my brother was in his second or third year of teaching and I just remember thinking that to be a Headteacher is the pinnacle of a teacher's career. I have never been the sort of person who settled at being just anything if I am honest, so I knew then that if I was going to be a teacher, I was going to be a Headteacher as that is where the profession culminates. I even had a career plan as an NQT – I knew I was going to leave schools in order to be a Head by the time I was forty. Almost every job I left, I was sad to leave, in fact I cried when I left but I had to take the next opportunity that came up. I got to Passmores as an Assistant Head and then before I knew it, I was Deputy Head and then the Head left and nobody else wanted the job! I remember standing there and thinking, 'I'm thirty-eight and I am the Head. How did that happen?' It was always in the career plan but not in that time. But in tough schools, there is never a queue to do the top job so that was it. I remember Steve Munby saying at a conference that being a new Head was like buying a new house; you write a list of all of the jobs that need doing and if you found that list seven years later, you would find that half of the jobs on the list weren't done. They weren't done because you either stopped noticing the cracks on the bathroom wall or you ran out of money. He said that if as a Head you stop noticing the cracks in the walls you need to stop being a Head at that school and go somewhere else. I have always had this speech in my mind – how long is too long? Am I still noticing the cracks? Am I still seeing what the community needs rather than what is comfortable to me? I think that is why I am still here as I am still seeing the cracks and that is why I have gone from Assistant Head to Deputy Head, to Head and now CEO of a Multi Academy Trust. There are always going to be times in your life when you ask yourself whether you're still good at and happy doing this or do you want to do something else. I am fifty-two now and probably reaching that point again.

Earlier in my career, I worked abroad for three years at a fee-paying international school in the middle of Cairo with brand new facilities like swimming pools, etc. It was lovely and the students were just gorgeous and were so thankful for the relationships they had with you. But I could have just walked in the classroom in September and given them a book and said, 'read that all day' and they would have done. As much as I loved the lifestyle and going diving every weekend, the fire for the job just wasn't there. So, I always knew that when I came back I was going to find a place which was more like me. I ended up in Harlow and it is very working class and a great place to raise aspirations which was definitely more like 'me.'

There have been so many significant moments in my career. Most of them have been quite small things but what has made them significant is the relationships I have with the people who make them significant. I remember about fifteen years ago, there was a young lady who was really hard work – she was as tough as they came. But I was determined to get her to come to prom because I knew that if I could get her to prom, I could make her realise that there was more to life than fighting and struggling. I wanted to show her that she could dress up and go to a nice place and be treated well. I remember seeing her at prom and just thinking, wow, she's here. It meant nothing to anyone else, but it meant everything to me to see her at that prom. It was a moment that I will always remember vividly. The most wonderful thing about this job is that there are daily versions of that. When you see a young person's behaviour change for the better because of something you have said or done, it is amazing. The job is tough and especially hard at the moment. When you stop and elevate yourself from all the rubbish we have to deal with, you realise what a privilege it is to have a purpose and that is the gift of the job.

One of the most tragic things I have experienced in my career was the loss of a pupil. We had a young man who had a heart condition and he passed away. When his cousin came into my office to tell me, I was so shocked and just felt complete and utter disbelief. I had only seen him the day before. He was one of those students that when you bumped into him, he made you feel better and he loved school. His parents asked if his coffin could come to the school on its way to the crematorium and of course I said yes. I will never forget it: on that day on the 16 December there were 1,200 students lining the road, in the rain, for twenty minutes in absolute silence. The message that gave to the community and the family. I am sure that those students will look back on that moment and reflect on what they did for that family. Walking in front of that hearse, past all the students stood in absolute silence, will live with me for ever.

In 2011, I was approached to film a documentary at the school by a production company. People say it was a brave decision but it wasn't, as we had no concept about what we were saying yes to! Every school that did it after us were the brave ones. To be honest, when we said yes, we thought we were doing a one-hour special, based out of school for 95% of it. Within days it had changed to a seven, or eight, part series filmed 99.9% in school! But it all came down to trust: I was sat at my desk with a producer opposite me telling us that they wanted to celebrate teachers and show the world how fantastic they are. How can you say no to that? I did tell the producer though, who was a lovely bloke, that if he damaged me, any of my staff or any of my kids that I would put him under a motorway. He looked at me and we locked eyes. He knew I was serious! He knew that if he broke our trust, he would never be able to work with any school again. I promised them that if they kept their word I would help them work with any of the schools they wanted to and they kept their word and so have I – every school that has had a series since I have visited the school and spoken to the Head. The governors made the decision that we would do the show and *Educating Essex* was born. At the time, we had no concept of how big it was going to be; I didn't think for one minute that I would be going to the pub on a Friday night and strangers would be asking me for selfies! That was odd as I am really a private person. I remember one day I was Christmas shopping with my son and a woman nearly fell off the escalator when she recognised me – so weird! My son was about seven or eight and he had no concept of what was going on, so was totally confused about why this woman was pointing at me and falling over. Even now, in year 13, if I do something on the news, he gets texts from his mates saying, 'I saw your dad on the telly!' I can't work out whether he is proud or not.

Educating Essex came at the perfect time. There had been lots of attempts to do reality shows in schools and they just weren't quite right. When they came to us, they realised that all they had to do was look inside the magic of this school and what they then found is that there is magic in every school.

But not everyone was happy that we got involved with the show. The day before the first episode had aired, I got a call from a chap from the Essex Education Board who told me we had to pull the series as it was going to damage the profession as he had received a call from the DfE saying that they were worried about it. He got quite nasty, calling me a disgrace and claiming that I was putting my own fame above children's lives. I held my resolve and at the end of year conference for Heads, when all the episodes had been aired, this man was retiring and one of the first things he said when he got on the podium was that he was sorry and that the show was the best thing that could have happened. I do understand why the powers that be were scared about the show as there are sometimes realities in a school that occassionally don't play out kindly for local authorities or the government. But these are the realities in school, so why are we hiding them?

Like most Headteachers, since the news that schools were closing last March due to the Covid-19 pandemic, there hasn't been an off switch yet. What I have been missing the most is that there is no longer an end to my day. At this time my working day starts when I open my eyes and it finishes when I close my eyes to go to bed. It is tough. There is an element of that relentlessness in the job anyway; if you are stupid enough to have emails on your phone or i-Pad, then you are never off work. I do have difficulties with this and having a switch off point is something I need to get to grips with but now is not the time. You need to be reactive especially knowing that on a regular basis, the government have been willing to give important announcements late on a Friday evening, with the expectation that we will get things put in place for Monday morning. This has been difficult. It means you are constantly in a state of hyper-alert and that is why it has been so tough and impossible to switch off. I am constantly reading everything I can to disseminate it to the staff. I email them every evening which includes my thoughts, or the daily news about what has happened in education that day and I will end it with a silly video or something. I have had so many staff telling me that they don't even bother to watch the news anymore – they just wait to get my emails because I will tell them the stuff they need to know, rather than all of the other stuff that is so depressing. The media, at times, seems to have a filter focussing on the negative perspectives and that is hard work when you are the focus of that negativity, which is what school staff have often been. I could just do with two days without emails, without being asked to make any decisions that I will have to impose. Just a few days of just doing my job would be helpful because it is so tiring.

In the first lockdown it was friends of the family that were dying. In the second lockdown it is parents and grandparents of the people you love. It is kids at the school losing their grandparents. My colleagues losing their parents. As a public person and a community leader you have a responsibility to be there for those moments as well. I have done too many funerals online this year and that takes its toll. It has gone from numbers being announced on the news to being, oh shit, that is my mate.

Teachers are good at problem solving. Covid testing in school hasn't bothered me – just give me the time and the equipment to set it up and I can do it. If it is possible, we can do it. That is the philosophy I have had through all of this, take your list and cross off all the impossible things on it, and you will be left with only the things which are possible. And don't worry about the things you have crossed off.

As the head of an organisation, it seems as though I spend all day making decisions for everyone else, and when I get home I just don't want to make any decisions at all. My wife can ask me the most simple question like, 'what shall we have for dinner?' I tell her to decide as I just can't face making another decision.

As a Headteacher, you try to give everybody the same time, empathy and compassion as sometimes you can get empathy fatigue. You cannot withdraw or isolate yourself in this moment as the responsibility is yours. Although you need to learn to rely on other people, this is the time when *you* need to make sure you take that responsibility. Though it can be easy to pull up the draw bridges staying connected is probably the healthiest thing.

If Covid-19 does not change education then we will have missed a massive opportunity. If there are key parts of our practice that do not evolve due to this pandemic, then we are fools. The use of online technology for training to free your staff up to go home at 15:30 – if we lose that then we are stupid. I think the lessons we are learning need to go to a listening government and we haven't got one of those. Why do we spend the afternoon of results day analysing what went wrong and what lessons we can learn for next year? It just doesn't seem that the government have done this. The things that need to change, like the high-stakes accountability, the funding and the assessment regime would take a reflective, mature and humble government. I am not sure any of those three words match the current government. I believe that individual schools and their staff will make the necessary changes about the things they want to change and the things they want to keep. Hopefully, these changes will be brilliant and will ripple out to a more national level and when we come out of the other side of this, these will be the positives we can draw from.

John Clifford

I am eighty-one years old and up until this year, I was still classroom teaching. Was I the oldest teacher in the UK? I am sure I read about somebody who is still teaching into their 90s... I was a Black Country boy and have stayed there to be a Black Country man. I went to Wednesbury Boy's High School and then onto Leeds University, where I read history. Both of my parents were teachers – my dad was a Primary Head and he came from farming stock in Worcestershire, starting out as a pupil teacher at only age fourteen. He was the youngest so didn't have the opportunity to become a farmer, so he tried his hand and never looked back.

Interestingly, both of my parents tried to put me off becoming a teacher; they didn't really regard teaching as a worthwhile career at the time! My godfather was a Pharmacist, so they wanted me to do that. I was all for it. But after my degree, I went to Leicester to do a PGCE and despite this, was determined still to not to go into teaching – but there was not much else around.

Doing a PGCE was quite uncommon at the time, and Leicester University was very progressive. The Senior Lecturer on the course was Robin Pedley, who wrote one of the first books on pedagogy and comprehensive education. They really were ahead of their time. This was in the post-war years, where quite a lot of teachers had been ex-soldiers – you didn't need a degree or higher qualifications, just a year at teacher training college.

The war had its effect throughout the 1950s, but there was more scope and optimism. When I was eighteen, I did some teaching in a tough secondary modern school. I really was shocked by what went on there. There was no permanent timetable and I was just sent to whatever class needed looking after at the time. One day, I was with another teacher and the kids were behaving quite well, there was a buzz of conversation, but they were also getting on with their work. The teacher I was with said "They are a right lot these. I'll show you how to deal with them." He shouted "Arthur!" and this big lad came lumbering out and he smacked him all around the room. There was no reason, he hadn't done anything wrong. He used him as an example as he was the biggest, to threaten the rest.

A couple of days later, I had to take the class on my own. It was a quiet reading lesson and there were no problems, so I was strolling up and down the gangways and went up behind Arthur and he was reading a comic under the desk. I stood behind him and he shoved his book out of sight swiftly, and his hands went up automatically to protect himself. I reassured him so he calmed down and I told him I couldn't read the *Beano*, as my parents didn't like it. This broke the ice and he told me he was reading the *Beano*, so I spoke to him nicely and he put it away and got the book he was supposed to be reading out. The next day, I was with the teacher who had hit Arthur and he walked beside us and gave me his old *Beano* magazines, saying "Here sir, I have finished with these." I was really touched by this and it shaped me for a long time.

This kind of behaviour from teachers was common in the 50s, it was the norm. Even I used the slipper when necessary, but I always tried to be fair. It was that military mentality which was left over from the war.

I started my high school education at Wednesbury Boy's High School and then ended up teaching there for fifty-nine years. I started my teaching career in 1959 and became the Head of History two years later, after the man who had taught me at school retired.

In 1967 the school became bilateral and joined up with a secondary modern school, later becoming Wood Green High School. The school doubled in size and due to this, I needed to re-apply for my own job. Luckily, I got it and held that position until the 1980s.

There were a lot of single sex schools when I started teaching, but in the 1970s, I found out what teaching girls was like. My whole approach had to change, and the popular military style and hitting etc. had to go. I have been lucky to only teach at one school where discipline is not a problem really, but it's still not easy. From the 1990s onwards, things definitely changed. Behaviour got better and you were able to actually teach. I think it was because the Head I was working with was keen on discipline and was quite forward looking. There was also a really strong SLT who were very experienced people, with the same vision, all working towards the same ends.

Nowadays, staying at the same school is almost unheard of, but I was happy where I was. I had loads of different opportunities over the years; while I was teaching, I was also doing youth work for Walsall Education Authority. I was very happy and didn't want to leave. In the 1980s, I became Head of Sixth Form and held this job down alongside being Head of History.

In the early 90s, the Head created a new job called Director of Community, to enhance the standing of the school in the local area, as it was going through a rough time. We needed some good PR, otherwise the school would close, as numbers were going down. We gradually built the school back up and then had our first Ofsted in the 90s: we came out very respectably.

Both myself and the Head retired in the 90s at the same time. I had worked under three heads in my career – the first was much older than me, then the last couple were the same age as me. People have asked me why I never wanted to be a headteacher, but I would have missed the classroom and that kind of interaction with the students.

When I retired, I was asked immediately if I would go back and do supply teaching. I jumped at the chance, as I hadn't really wanted to retire but it became sensible to do so; I was offered redundancy money and a lump sum, and it would have been silly not to accept it. I certainly wasn't ready to stop teaching though, so I went back to school for two days a week. I knew this would be good for me and I was happy to do it; it meant I kept in touch with people, which was important to me.

I have been at the school for such a long time that I have seen people leave and come back again. I have acres of experience and I believe it is a great asset. I remember looking up to more experienced teachers when I was younger. They knew how to do things and that spread to younger teachers and we could talk to them and get good advice. There is a new phenomenon at the moment of appointing very young, inexperienced Heads who haven't served their time in the classroom. I feel this is one of the things which is wrong about teaching. The best teachers often get promoted very quickly, which takes them out of the classroom. This is ridiculous! That's where it is going wrong as that's where I have always been happiest.

Obviously, teaching for so long means that I have witnessed a great many changes in the profession and each change I have gone through has been a great trial for teachers. The powers that be got uptight and it seems like there was change for the sake of change. A lot of these changes brought little positive results and just succeeded in panicking people. I am afraid I got quite cynical. I used to say to colleagues, "Don't worry! If it's going to succeed it will succeed." It was disruptive; a lot of teachers felt changes were brought in for box ticking and it detracted from what was really important. This is still the case.

One of the biggest changes I witnessed in teaching was the introduction of the National Curriculum. Of course, it's good for teaching to have some element of containment, as the discipline of a curriculum is important, so nationally we all focus on the same thing. But it hindered me, as I felt I wanted to experiment and was bound when the National Curriculum came in. I even argued about the way I felt with an HMI Inspector, telling him that we are curbed, and he agreed. Of course, it could be helpful for some teachers to be directed in that way. I was resentful of it at the time, although I can now see the benefits, but I do still hear teachers complaining about it. My strength is communicating, and I felt that some of that had been taken away by the prescribed nature of what we all now had to teach.

Some of the younger teachers I have worked with now don't communicate in the same way that we were brought up to do. I believe in talking to kids, in sharing things with them about me and my background and now this has been replaced by a drive for results. When I retired, I took a GCSE class and one of the boys told me that the teacher they normally had never really spoke to them as he was always on his computer. I found this really sad. I am on a pub quiz team with four ex-pupils now and have become friends with many kids I have taught over the years. This only happened because the students felt they knew and trusted me.

Yet workload is so crazy now that teachers sometimes don't have the time to fully get to know the kids. Teachers are expected to do an insane amount of stuff that isn't actually teaching, such as filling in forms, etc. I find that very trying. Data is especially awful; I can't see the point of most of it, reams and reams of paper! But then, I am a dinosaur now I suppose! I see younger teachers who are almost crucified by it. They are staying up until 2 a.m. most nights doing planning and marking, endless evidencing that they are doing their jobs and then they burn out. It is no surprise that some aim to move to SLT quickly, to escape the pressure of classroom teaching.

Personal experiences inevitably change the way you teach. Having children of your own changes you, as you want them to be taught properly and in turn think about your own teaching. I have always believed in taking the positives from negative experiences, as it makes you stronger as a person if you face up to the nastier things in life. I have witnessed younger teachers crumpling very quickly to any pressure. I think it is probably a generational thing in society. I was a war baby and although I didn't really realise what was happening, I witnessed terrible situations.

My father was in the forces and we were all extremely upset at him being sent to the Far East. I remember him coming home and luckily, he didn't end up going. Even though we were not always aware of the horror of things, silent conversations were always there, and we just accepted it. We always knew someone who had experienced something awful and this just prepared you for the worst. I remember finding spent shells, going into the air raid shelter and having to wear gas masks. Hearing bombers above the Midlands was terrifying and I still remember the sound of the drone. Perhaps the younger generation have been sheltered too much? I don't know. We had to be a fairly resilient generation; even though we missed the worst of it that our parents and grandparents had to put up with, we still had that knowledge and fear. Living through the Cold War was also pretty traumatic, as we felt that it might all be happening again. But this time worse – atomic war. It all builds up an ability to accept things more readily than others.

My father once told me a story about when he was growing up during the First World War. He was working on the farm and had to escort two German prisoners of war from the camp to the farm to do some work. He was only ten and was given a rifle! He then had to escort them back. Being old like I am, you get those generational stories that help to put your own worries and experiences into perspective. Unfortunately, when generations die out, that valuable source of history dries up as well.

I have been a teacher for a long time, and I hope I am remembered as a human teacher, in that I have a love and compassion for young people. It is this which has inspired me to carry on as long as I have. I haven't done any teaching in the last year and I miss it. Young people are so inspiring in themselves that they inspire me. They have kept me young by their sheer madness and their daftness – there is a lot of joy in seeing them being ridiculous. You have to be prepared to listen to what they have to say, as they have a lot of interesting things to say which are well worth listening to!

In the last year, school supply budgets have been cut back, so it's unlikely I will go back. But if it weren't for this, I would have carried on this year, even though I am not as fit as I was. I still go in and see them and I would love to go back. I am eighty-one years old and I don't think I will ever fully retire. Once a teacher, always a teacher.

Dan Morrow

I grew up in the Medway Towns, raised by my amazing mum. She worked very hard with four different cleaning jobs and instilled a strong work ethic in myself and my brother. I went to a great Primary School in Gillingham and didn't realise at the time how disadvantaged it was. I was the only one in my year group of sixty who passed the 11+ and so went on to one of the Grammar Schools in Rochester.

It was a different world. One where I was now the only child on free school meals, not one of many. It was frightening sometimes to feel such an outsider, but I was determined to try my hardest and achieve. I got straight 'A' grades and then went to Oxford University and studied Modern History.

Once again, I felt excluded – I had the brains but not the money, as my Nan used to say to me.

By the time I got to the end of my degree, I decided that I wasn't going to pursue my dream of becoming a teacher – I wanted money! Not just for me, but to provide for the rest of my family also.

I joined KPMG on a fast track to partnership scheme and worked as an auditor across the entertainment sector. I then joined Disney as an Assistant Accountant and got to work on *Harry Potter and the Prisoner of Azkaban*. From there, I went on to work on a number of films, including *Pirates of the Caribbean*, *National Treasure*, *The Holiday* and *Kinky Boots*. It was a different world yet again but one where I, surprisingly, was no longer excluded. The pay was very generous indeed and at the age of twenty-six, I was able to buy my mum a house and then make a change for myself.

There is no doubt that the film industry is hard work, fun, exciting and a little crazy. Let's face it, it is pretty cool to have your name at the end of a film! I had the pleasure of working with creative and interesting people who were part of something truly magical. Yet, I knew it wasn't quite me. I really did enjoy it; getting to travel and be on location, getting to mingle with the cast and attend premieres – what is not to like? But I wanted what I now have – the opportunity to make an impact on social justice, to be a voice and a role model for others, to bring equity. What a privilege.

My grandad had passed his 11+ when he was a child, but because he wore clogs and came from a family that could not afford to compete, he was excluded. When I got my grammar school place, I did not get a free bus pass. It used to cost £1.60 a day for me to go to school and when my brother later joined the same school, it meant that just getting us to and from school took 25 per cent of my mum's income. My grandparents helped where they could, but there was no doubting that our education came at a great personal cost. It wasn't until I was thirteen or fourteen that I realised that my mum wasn't just "not hungry," she was purposefully going without. That in itself took a toll on her health.

My grandad told both my brother and I that we had one job to do; to ensure we "hold the ladder." Clogs meant he hadn't gotten onto the rung himself, but he would proudly insist that he bought our school shoes each year and helped us take that step. Our job was to ensure that we then held that ladder for others like us, to climb too.

Now, don't get me wrong. This doesn't mean I am a big grammar school fan – I'm not. For my success story, so clearly based on the sacrifices of others, there were fifty-nine other children in my primary school who didn't get the same opportunities. Many were bright and sparky, but from lower Gillingham, where expectations for education at the time were just not that strong.

In the year that I achieved my GCSEs, the majority of my primary friends attended a local failing secondary that posted a seven per cent pass rate with English and Maths; I felt so much shame and guilt about this injustice and unfairness. As a consequence of this, at twenty-six, I retrained. I took a large pay cut and begun the Graduate Teacher Program as a history teacher, in a highly challenging secondary in Croydon. I loved every minute and I still do.

My grandfather wasn't the only reason I wanted to retrain; I was also privileged to have the most incredible teachers. At primary school, the head teacher was a man called Jim Fernie. His care for the whole community and high expectations were different from the norm. He bought books for me to keep and nurtured a love of English and history in me. He always ensured that the boys at the school who didn't have dads at home had a role model to aspire to.

Then at secondary school, my history teacher was called Keith Baker. He was the type of grammar school teacher who feels part of the fabric of the school, as if he was a living embodiment of the institution. He was erudite and interesting and debated with me as if I had already completed a degree, challenging me to be the best version of myself.

One day, I sat with him at the end of Lower Sixth and explained that I was not going to apply to university as I wanted to find an entry-level job so that I could contribute at home. He looked me in the eye and said: "My dear boy, you will not just be going to any university, you will attend Oxford and in doing so your mum will burst with pride."

He was right. I applied and to my surprise was offered a place. He gave me music to listen to, literature to read and he and his wife even had me round for dinner and explained to me how the cutlery would work, what wine was and gave me my first olive... I wasn't an initial fan but am now quite the convert! He saw potential in me, but also recognised the barriers that would be in my way.

My ethos is this: every learner has an invisible backpack and within are their experiences and events that have occurred in their life. For some, this is their cultural capital, their key. Often, in more disadvantaged or challenging areas, this backpack can be filled with issues, problems and at times, traumas. I believe as an educator, our role first and foremost is to give children the confidence, self-esteem and voice to begin to understand how they can empty that pack and refill it with what they need. I believe in giving children agency. I believe in children.

My name is Dan and I am the Trust Leader for a family of primary schools in South East London and North Kent. I became a teacher because if I can positively impact on children, in even a small way, in the same way I was impacted on, then I will see my life as fulfilling.

Caroline Spalding

I come from a long line of teachers: my grandparents were headteachers, my dad was a Headteacher and my mum was an Assistant Headteacher and they all loved it. So, essentially, I have grown up in schools around people who were really positive about education and devoted to their jobs. They are amazing people – my grandad even got an OBE for his charity work focused on supporting children with special educational needs and my dad worked at the same school for twenty-one years. When you see the kind of impact that makes on young people and the wider community, it is pretty hard not be sucked into it.

But, saying that, when I went to university being a teacher wasn't a done deal. I remember I had aspirations to be a barrister or work in the law, but I finished my degree and thought to myself 'is that really what I want to do?' So, I did some work experience at my dad's school and I think I just knew on the first day that teaching was what I wanted to pursue; teenagers are hilariously funny and I just had so much fun that I never really looked back.

Since day one I think I've known that at some point I want to be a headteacher, but all the people I value as heads have done it quite late in their career, so it would never be something I would rush into. The job is totally knackering. Why would you want to get there sooner? My dad was only a Head in the last ten years of his career as he has always said you need to learn your craft. I mean, who wants to be a crap Head?! I've learned the importance of taking your time and making sure you are good at what you do before you seek progression.

Education is about people and transforming local communities and I have always felt part of the local communities that I have worked in. I bought my first flat on the same road as my current school. I never thought I would end up staying in Derby my whole life, but I love it here and am very happy. If I can become a Head in Derby that would be brilliant. I love my current school, although it was a big change from where I had come from. Around 60 per cent of our pupils speak English as an additional language and I was a bit like a rabbit in the headlights when I first arrived. Despite having taught English for over ten years, at first I felt like an NQT again.

Soon after I'd started, I had to conduct a GCSE Speaking and Listening assessment with my year 11 class. A girl chose to speak about her experiences in Sri Lanka during the civil war there. She described the most harrowing atrocities she had witnessed to an audience of kids that couldn't have been more culturally diverse: a white British boy, a Romany gypsy girl, a Pakistani Muslim boy and me. We all just sat there completely speechless. None of us knew what to say. She finished and the Roma girl turned to me and said, "This will be in my heart forever." She was so touched by what she had heard. One of the lads said "Our school is amazing isn't it miss? All communities together." It sounds so cheesy now but it has stayed with me years later. If communities could just come together and have these conversations, the world would be a better place. That girl went on to do an opening keynote for me at a WomenEd event and has just started university. I am so proud of her and her achievements.

Working with children over the last fourteen years I guess I just assumed my husband and I would have our own children at some point. We had one pregnancy end at 14 weeks shortly before we were due to return to school after the holidays. Then we just couldn't seem to get pregnant again. This time last year, we began preparations for IVF. We were so excited, particularly when we finally got the delivery that went straight into our fridge. I started to psych myself up for giving myself the injections, then on the first day the injections were due to start the lockdown was announced and the clinic then rang us up and basically said "Stop! Don't do it!"

We finally began our cycle at the start of the summer term as the first national lockdown began to lift. We were so lucky that our first round ended up working, which we never expected! It felt pretty miraculous if I am honest. Of course, we've now been left worrying that I might give birth during a lockdown as well, which is still touch and go at the moment.

Throughout this whole thing, my school has been amazing. My Head is incredible; if you wanted a perfect example of how somebody should behave, he is it. A normal pregnancy during normal times is a hormonal rollercoaster but being pregnant after difficulty in conceiving and in a global pandemic has certainly been interesting!

I like having certainty and you think that medical staff have all the 'answers'. I believed that they would be able to tell me you are either safe to be in school while pregnant, or you're not. But that guidance has never been given. I am now, at this time, thirty-four weeks pregnant and I will still be going in to school on Monday. As pregnant women are not classed as 'clinically extremely vulnerable' it is at the school's discretion and if a risk assessment is in place it is considered that there is no reason you can't go in.

My Headteacher has been really understanding and from the outset has said that I need to talk to him about how I feel and tell him any adaptations I feel I need. At first, I found that a bit intimidating as I just wanted to be guided and I felt like it put a lot of pressure on me to choose. But now, six months down the line, when I have made lots of choices, I feel the Head has empowered me to choose what feels right for me and my family. I don't do any face-to-face teaching and I am not on the on-call rota. If I choose to go into school, it is because I have made the choice to go in. There are certain meetings I want to be involved in and I think now, that if that choice had been taken away, I would find that really disempowering, so I have come full circle. The lack of clarity has been hard though.

One of the toughest moments was the realisation at Christmas that I probably wouldn't get to teach in person again before the baby was born. It upset me that I wouldn't get to say goodbye to my year 11s. I have a Key Stage 4 role on the Senior Leadership Team and we were robbed of the chance to say a proper goodbye to our year 11 last year as well. Our school has only ever had a prom in the last couple of years. I teach in an area with a high level of deprivation and we were given the local University's students' union for free as a venue for the prom. All the kids were so excited, so we were all gutted when we had to cancel it. Not being able to say a proper goodbye again is a tough pill to swallow and, I'm not going to lie, I had a bit of a cry about it. I'm not sure my husband got it, to be honest!

Sometimes those not in teaching don't fully understand the bonds we make with the students. Last term, I remember one lad pausing and giving me a funny look when I was in the middle of teaching the class a poem before he quietly said, "Miss you've got two sets of legs and two sets of arms." The penny had clearly just dropped that he meant I was carrying a baby. I feel like I have shared a lot of the journey with them. Even the IVF journey too; I went into a Science lesson where I showed them all the photos and told them all about my experience. Of course, I have promised I will bring my daughter in at some point to show them – I have got to. During covid I am also still ringing some kids I mentor on a weekly basis, so it has been so nice to still hear their voices and they've been genuinely concerned about me, asking how I am doing, etc. It is really quite sweet!

Yet, I do realise how lucky I am to work in a school. What about the pregnant women working in supermarkets and other key worker positions who wouldn't have had anywhere near as many safeguarding measures put in place that I have? I have had choice and autonomy, which I recognise is such a privileged position to be in.

During this andemic, a lot of people have been calling for there to be drastic changes in education but I'm less keen for any kind of 'revolution' and would rather we just focused on incremental improvement. Due to my family history and the fact I have been teaching a long time, I have always tried to see the long view. I have constantly heard my dad say "Oh, we have done this before" or "That's come round again." I think that is really healthy, as teaching can be a political football and, honestly, it shouldn't be.

It has been interesting to get to grips with teaching live lessons online and the way it boils teaching down to its essentials – in many ways ignoring much of the noise and rubbish that is so often foisted on schools. For me the fundamentals are the transmission of knowledge and the relationships we build with pupils and the community within which we are working. I hope that doesn't change.

What I do hope changes is that there is more recognition of how important education and our profession is. I'm sure that home schooling will have given many parents a new perspective on it!

And, of course, I hope the same thing happens to our amazing NHS. Our public services are so vital and yet historically have been chronically under-funded and under-appreciated.

Maybe some good will come out of the last year after all. One bright light being that people will really value those of us working in our public services.

Sarah Dearden

Starting my career as a teacher during a global pandemic was not really part of the plan...but I didn't really have a conventional path to teaching anyway.

I was born and bred in a tiny village on the Pennines called Greenfield, one of the villages of Saddleworth. I loved village life and totally embraced being part of the community but I always wanted a taste of working in the city and longed to have an exciting career which would challenge me to the best I could be.

I initially went to university to study Law, with the plan of becoming a solicitor and while I was at university, I got really involved in 'Street Law,' which is a charitable organisation that aims to empower people with legal and civic knowledge through education programs. I volunteered to become a school's coordinator, which meant I went into deprived schools to work with them. I went into a school in Denton in Manchester and did a lot of work with them on stop and search and the legalities behind when you can be stopped and searched and when you can refuse. I loved the experience and felt really passionate about it, so the first seeds of becoming a teacher were planted, but I still wasn't sure. With this in mind, I decided to go travelling after university and thought that when I came back I would be ready to become a solicitor. I got back and secured a job at a law firm but after a year of working there, I just felt like my soul was squashed…I felt like a shadow of the person I was. I decided to quit but I am still not sure when I made that decision that teaching was for me as none of my family are teachers. All I knew was that I needed to fill that void that had been created by sitting in a corporate office environment for a year. After researching what teaching was like, it felt like something I wanted to do. It was then that I met another trainee teacher who had also been a solicitor for many years and was also changing careers. She told me to go for it and this was really the deciding factor for me, as she had been through it all and was happy with her decision.

Before I started my training year, I spent some time working in a tough school in Oldham in Greater Manchester as a Teaching Assistant. The behaviour was so bad at the school that at times it was like a zoo! The school was going through a lot of changes and my experience there threw up a few doubts as the staff seemed to have no control over the students at all. There was a lot of disgruntled staff who were just fed up of the way the school was being run, but there was also a lot of incredibly dedicated and passionate staff, who were very inspirational. When I started my SCITT training, this school wanted me to stay and do my first placement there but I was against this as I wanted a fresh start. I didn't want the kids to see my transition from the TA sat at the back to becoming a classroom teacher. I did enjoy my time at this school though and learnt so much. It was so rewarding – particularly the relationships I built with some of the kids. Some of their circumstances were just unbelievable and I felt I was genuinely making a difference. When you can be that safe place for a child, I realised that this was the career I had been looking for.

As an Oldham girl, it seemed strangely inevitable that I might end up working at the school I attended as a pupil. But when they told me I was going there for my second placement I thought 'No!! Anywhere but there!" I felt sick with anxiety about it as I was at a point in my life where it didn't feel like progress, it felt like going backwards. I had worked really hard to break into the law world and leaving it made me feel a bit of a failure, wondering what I had worked for. But I definitely think having some time in industry has been a positive in my teaching career, particularly when it comes to perspective. There is no doubt that teaching has a tough workload but when I was working as a paralegal, I worked longer hours for less money. Now I have the freedom of holidays and I really appreciate them. My former career also taught me a lot about how to compartmentalise and have a work life balance; I was working on some really distressing cases and I had to learn to switch off for my own wellbeing. Sometimes teaching can seem relentless, so this has really helped me. I also think that in other jobs, I have always been bored and felt stuck in a rut. I have never felt like this as a teacher as every day is different and there are so many options for career progression, so I feel fulfilled professionally.

I live in the school community, so when I first went back to my old school, I was worried about how that might fit with teaching in it. I worried whether I would constantly bump into the kids or know some of the parents...I had never been bothered about having a drink in the village but now I wondered whether I would have to move as I would feel so uncomfortable! But I needn't have worried. I was delighted when they offered me my NQT position during my placement and I love working here.

In the first few months, there were some tough days but by Christmas, I felt like I was just getting into my stride and things were beginning to get easier. I had a year 10 class that had a lot of special educational needs and I felt like I was making real progress with them and building relationships, then all of a sudden we got the announcement that school was closing due to Covid-19 and my NQT year, as I knew it, was cut short. It was pretty disorientating for me – like it was for any teacher. But as a new teacher, you rely so much on the support and validation of your more experienced colleagues, so the prospect of not having that was initially worrying. Remote learning was in its infancy in my school, so it seemed a bit like we had lost touch with one another for a while. But I had a brilliant mentor and the support of another NQT in the department; we ended up speaking on the phone every day and he kept me busy with planning schemes of work and collaborating on video lessons, so I was never in the position of sitting there with nothing to do. During this time, I continued to teach a full timetable, managing my own classes and providing regular feedback. I can honestly say, that without that, I would have been at a complete loss. My colleagues definitely got me through it.

Perhaps one of the biggest challenges I had was not being able to develop proper relationships with the pupils in my care. I would pose them questions in our online groups or message them but sometimes it felt like it was disappearing into the ether a bit. It was a bizarre situation; one that we were all getting used to and getting to grips with. It was the same when I provided feedback. Every time I spent hours writing it, I wondered whether my students were even reading it at all. It was all so different from the way I would usually work in the classroom, where I would be able to see the impact of the feedback I gave and witness the pupils improve. Even managing the feedback on top of everything else was a struggle. At first we were giving students individualised feedback on three pieces of work each, every single week. In school, we would give lots of verbal feedback but probably only mark work once a fortnight, so the marking load was much heavier. Later on, we changed to whole class feedback, which was much more manageable but I did still wonder whether they were even looking at it.

Another thing I struggled with was the uncertainty. When would we return? We were spending a lot of time writing new schemes of learning but I couldn't envisage a time we would be teaching them face-to-face or even if we would. I was putting my heart and soul into planning these lessons but didn't know when or if they would ever be used. I suppose every teacher was feeling the same but they had the wisdom of years of practice, whereas I had only been teaching a few months so I needed the routine and regularity of school to keep me grounded.

Looking back, I sometimes think about the lost opportunities from my NQT year: the CPD, the feedback and the opportunity to observe other colleagues. The toughest thing though was having to find your feet again when I returned to the classroom as it just felt that bit more difficult. I realise how fortunate I was to have that support though, as I never really felt adrift and I could have done! Although completing my training year in a pandemic was definitely not in the plan, I feel like I have learnt so much from it and my experiences have definitely shaped the kind of teacher I want to become.

I am now enjoying my second year of being back in the classroom. Of course, we have still had disruptions but there has at least been periods of normality. I was slightly apprehensive about returning but all that disappeared as soon as the first class was in front of me. This summer will also bring additional challenges as I will have to formulate GCSE teacher assessed grades for my two year 11 classes. The process is so confusing that I do feel a level of anxiety but it is only because I know I need to do a good job and give them what they deserve. Despite all of this I love my job and I couldn't imagine doing anything else.

Matthew Milburn

I was fortunate to be taught by some brilliant teachers. One that really stands out was Robin Fairchild who taught Geography at my secondary school. On one of my reports he wrote "an able boy who knows it." To be fair, that probably summed me up quite well at the time. I was cocky, awkward and probably not particularly pleasant as a young teenager trying to find my way. Rather than give up on me or be dismissive, he invested in me and showed faith. He put me in *The Mikado* – one of Gilbert and Sullivan's operettas and I found my voice through performing. This production was a turning point in my life. I went on to do Theatre Studies at A-Level and was successful in auditions for Surrey Youth Theatre. Eventually I went on to study a degree in Drama and History.

I knew I wanted to teach and did my PGCE at Birmingham with David Davis who had a profound influence on me. Some teachers speak about their training year as being unhelpful but mine was hugely formative - David really inspired me. He instilled in me an interest in experiential learning and I became a firm believer in the educational power of living through moments of drama more so than performance theatre; much of my work has been about children living through and learning from a moment. We learn more powerfully from what we enjoy, when we feel motivated, so making learning as playful as we can means it is more fun and students want to do it. The motivation becomes theirs', they are not just doing it because "miss tells you that you must."

During my training I worked in some great inner-city schools in Birmingham and my first job was at Breeze Hill School in Oldham. I worked closely with Neil Clark who was Head of Languages and Harkireet Sohel who was a history and drama teacher. Together we sought to facilitate inspirational experiences for students, such as visiting the D-Day landing beaches and going to Berlin just after the wall came down. Pupils would perform theatre in education with the second language woven in to the text. Neil and I moved together to work at Oldham Sixth Form College and I taught A-Levels and a blended GCSE course that included drama, media and English. After a few years I was made Assistant Principal.

After serving six years as a curriculum Deputy Head in Leeds, in 2003 I was made Headteacher at Kingstone School in Barnsley. We developed cultural studies and 'Assessment for Living' as a form of assessment, which were all based on this idea of living through moments, rather than just writing about them or reading them in a book. The school became a School of Creativity and in 2011, I started as Head at Saddleworth School where I remained until I retired from teaching in 2020, in the midst of the Covid-19 pandemic.

My philosophy has always centred around seeking to empower and inspire staff and students. Students should be able to find their voice. The more I reflect on my career, the more I realise that it is also about finding purpose; if a child feels motivated and interested then they are going to learn...if a student can find that innate purpose and motivation, then even the most distant and dry learning becomes easy. It is about finding what is meaningful to that young person which is the key to unlocking the learning. It's because of this belief that we developed the Pupil Driven Review process at Saddleworth, where young people get the chance to share with an audience of their parents/carer, a teacher and some of their peers, what they have learnt, where they want to go and how the adults in their life can enable them to get to where they want to be. It isn't always easy for teenagers to open up and explain their thoughts; if you don't ask them the questions, many won't give you the answer. Schooling should be much more responsive than it is and one of the reasons that I wanted to leave early is because I felt it was getting more and more distant. I hope that the Coronavirus pandemic enables us to re-examine what the experience of the child is like. In my view, we can't just plough on with this knowledge-heavy curriculum, regardless of where the learner is up to. We have got to stop and ask the students how they are and what they are interested in learning about. The teacher's skills is then to act on this understanding for the class and for the individual student together. In my view the current system of assessment is completely broken and should be replaced. It is nothing more than a grading system that has very little to do with assessment in its true sense. It is like a factory process where the outcome is just a number or a grade. Even OfQUAL recognise that this grade could be one or two grades out depending on a whole range of variables on the day the student sits the paper. There are far more effective and educative ways of assessing students that allow the students to feel empowered and to offer a self-evaluation of how they are progressing. It was trying to pursue this more child-centred approach that motivated me as a Head; trying to encourage students and their families to be involved in assessment and encouraging the child to have a voice and find that motivation for what it is that they want to learn. I am not of course suggesting that there is not key knowledge that students need to learn but we need to look at the whole of the curriculum and consider why we don't teach things like politics and philosophy or personal finance, but we do teach Pythagoras in Maths and Moles in Science. Of course, those things can be useful but I do think it is time for us to look at the curriculum afresh and think about how we can make it more relevant, attractive and purposeful for young people.

As we progress through teaching, we should be helping to humanise young people so that they understand the preciousness of life. It is for the adults to help young people come to terms with what life means. In 2015, a Year 7 pupil tragically passed away and having provided space for the children to grieve, we asked those who wished to, to line up for a guard of honour, as his cortége passed down the main street of the village where the school is located. We wanted to show the young people how significant this was and for it to be a moment where our school community came together. It was a moment to acknowledge the tragedy but also to recognise what an incredible life this young man had. We also used to come together as a school to mark Remembrance Day. To see the students and staff fall silent and remember all of those who had lost their lives, to suddenly hear the bird song, was incredibly powerful and moving – a genuine moment of awe and wonder. There are those in education who would argue that school time is too precious; that there would be too much 'lost learning' for students to do those things during school time. But it is these things that truly humanise a child, that educate the soul and shape them as people.

Of course, being a Headteacher isn't just about these incredible moments. There are many, many challenges and in recent years the myopic focus on exam performance has in my view become damaging. Exam scores have become the only barometer of success and the system has bred a series of what I would term 'perverse behaviours' from Heads. There is an obsession with driving for grades, to the point where nothing else matters and I find that offensive. Education is about human development in its broadest sense – not just the very narrowest brilliance that a student can show at GCSE or A-Level. There is no doubt that there are Headteachers who game the system and there were moments where we were put under incredible pressure to do the same. I know of Headteachers who have taken large numbers of students off roll, just prior to the census. These were children who weren't going to do very well in their exams. They were then put back on roll just after the census so they didn't count in the official figures. I am not blaming these colleagues; it is the fault of the system. In the past I used ECDL scores to top up grades and make the school look better. The pressure on Headteachers is immense; it comes from the academy chain, the local authority, the governing body, who in turn feel the heat from central government. It is all about game theory: we need to know how well our schools are doing so we need to compare one school with another, compare one student with another and see which is the better school. This is far too simplistic because schools are incredibly complex organisations that deal in humanity. Dealing with human emotions is completely different to five A*-C in English and Maths or Progress 8. What we should be looking at is how successful a school is at helping a young person to grow, develop and become a more rounded adult, who has academic opportunity as well as a healthy sense that this isn't the be all and end all. Balancing this was the biggest challenge I faced. Throughout my seventeen years of Headship, the goal posts changed so many times on what we were being judged against.

I had already decided that I would be retiring from teaching at the end of the academic year in 2020 and I didn't imagine that I would be doing so in such extraordinary circumstances. A colleague who has family in China had been telling me that the Covid-19 virus was going to be huge and that we needed to prepare. I remember being completely naive about it and saying to him "let's just wait." Then I remember, after the news had come through on the Wednesday that we would be closing and changing to an online learning platform, standing at the gate on the Friday and saying goodbye to the children. Actually, because I was retiring in July of that year, this turned out to be the last day where we had a full group in school. It was peculiar. At this point, I was the Executive Head and I sat down with the Head and we began to work out how we were going to handle this unprecedented situation. At that stage there were a lot of scared people. We had a staff of just over 130 and we wanted to be able to respond to the reality of the situation as they felt it. When we were instructed that we needed to invite key worker and vulnerable children back into school, we set up a rota, with staff who were comfortable about coming into school and teaching these groups. We tried to just listen to staff and trust them. The team all rallied together and my colleagues on SLT also designed a home learning plan and with the help of the ICT technicians team, got Teams up and running and trained the staff on the Teams platform within a matter of days. It was extraordinary to see how quickly staff adapted to it. Then there was the logistics of making the school safe for the students who were coming in for face-to-face teaching: moving all of the tables and chairs out, so that there was only six students in each class – which was the guidance at the time, having check points where staff and students could wash their hands and keeping class bubbles separate. We worked in partnership with one of our local primary schools and they used part of our school building.

It was an intense period of uncertainty and I know colleagues found it extremely difficult to switch off. Having been a Head for seventeen years, I had learned to compartmentalise more successfully. This means working hard each day but then knowing that, once at home, mentally breaking away from work and living in the moment with family and friends. Like many people, I did end up drinking more than I had done previously and put on some weight and for me, these are fairly obvious signs that things were not as balanced as I wanted them to be. As well as being the Executive Head, I was also a National Leader of Education and thankfully, all of that work dried up so what was helpful was that I was able to focus my time working with the Head. Together we drove forward with the systems and communication that needed to be tight if we were to navigate such an uncertain period.

Towards the end of the first lockdown, when schools were asked to open more widely to some Key Stage 4 pupils, we met with the members of staff individually who had not felt able to come to school since March. We felt that now would be the time to invite them back in as we didn't want them to feel isolated. Online video meetings are great but it isn't the same as the collegiate atmosphere that you get when you are actually in school with your colleagues. We had been having socially distanced staff briefings every day for this reason; every day there was a new team of staff coming in so we wanted to just remind people that they were part of something bigger than themselves.

There were some truly extraordinary contributions from staff. The Teaching Assistants did so much for students and their families who were struggling through the pandemic, including putting food parcels together and delivering them around Oldham. Just amazing.

There were many, many challenges during this time. On one occasion during the Covid-19 outbreak, we had a young man who was going around spitting on door handles. This was the reaction of a child who was confused and perplexed about what was going on in the world. It was a symbolic moment because how you deal with that is indicative of how you view children. There are schools that would have immediately permanently excluded that child, but having learned from the great drama teacher Dorothy Heathcote, we always look at education as a crucible, where you are constantly stirring up knowledge and working with the student and questioning them to say, "I wonder why it looks like that?" They can then explain their behaviours.

No amount of experience could have prepared any of us for what happened with our dear colleague Barrie Ashley. Barrie had been working as a caretaker at the school for a number of years and everybody loved him: students, the local community and school staff. He was brilliantly flamboyant with a love of fashion and music. He loved going on holiday to Malta every year and towards the end of each term, he would be on a countdown until he could go and relax and enjoy himself in the sun, telling any staff who would listen that it wasn't long now until he was "off!" For the last few years, Barrie had held a pivotal role in the school panto. Murray Lucas would try and direct him as he sang and danced on the stage with uninhibited joy. The students would erupt in rapturous applause, thrilled that "our Barrie" was yet again the star of the show. He loved white clothing and the year before, had attended the prom for the first time looking fabulous in a white suit. His renditions of popular 70s disco classics often floated in through classroom windows, as he sang away while brushing up the courtyards and he always had time for a "hello" or quick chat with anyone – staff, student or visitor.

In April 2020, Barrie became ill and was admitted to hospital. He was in his 60s and had some underlying health conditions, but he had an active job and was physically able, so although we were concerned, we were optimistic. It became increasingly clear that

Barrie was very ill and, unfortunately, he passed away - another victim of the Coronavirus pandemic. I spoke to his brother, who was incredibly kind, dignified and generous and he told us that Barrie had died with him by his side on a screen/phone and not in person, as he was not allowed to be with him in his last moments. It devastated the school; he was the type of character that every school needs.

We wanted to get a message out as soon as we could to colleagues, so that everybody found out at the same time, but obviously we needed to see if this was acceptable to his family, as it was their news to share. They confirmed that I could and I drafted the difficult message to staff that "our Barrie" had sadly passed away. I won't ever forget the avalanche of emails that came from so diverse a range of staff – you could hear the voice of the contributors in each of the stories and memories they were sharing. They were all very heart-felt and genuine. A day or so after the news, an ex-student and an Art teacher produced a stunning collage, made up with students and staff's faces, which made up Barrie's face when they were put together. We also knew we had to do something as a school to mark Barrie's passing, but many of the usual things we might do were out of the question due to social distancing and covid restrictions. We knew that the cortége would be passing the school, so we bought white roses and children in school made them up into buttonholes and gave them out to those lining the street. As the car passed the school, I gave a card to his brother through the window, which had the collage on the front. It was important for the students to be able to mark this moment and to remember; not to be sentimental about it but to understand that this was the end of a life – let's acknowledge that in an appropriate way.

During this time there was some very touching and poignant tributes for Barrie: some students had grown plants and written notes, poems and letters, or decorated pebbles and left them outside the school. I don't think there was another colleague who would have elicited that response from those children and staff alike. He was the first person I had known who had died from covid – if indeed that was what he actually died from. It brought it very close to home. It was terribly sad and he had an incredible life. I hope one day that we are all able to go to the local rugby club and celebrate his life – perhaps all wearing tight white jeans and dancing like nobody is watching.

I think Covid-19 will change many things in society and I hope that the exam system in England is one of them. I hope we can design a more rounded process for assessing children, one that also involves parents and is more inclusive; one that is more about what children can do, not what they cannot do. However, I suspect this will be a difficult shift to make. Universities are at the top of the food-chain and they still want grades. Many universities don't even interview students for places any more. It is just a number crunching exercise. It seems to make much more sense for a student to have, e.g. a portfolio of learning and then to be interviewed about these pieces of work, so you get a much more rounded view. I appreciate that this would be time consuming but it would be a more credible and accurate view of where a human being is up to.

Being a teacher and a Headteacher is a privilege and it gave me an incredible purpose but it did not define me and I think in the best teachers, work doesn't define them. They know how important it is and they don't do it half-heartedly. That said, this pandemic should be a reminder of how precious life is. When it's 4 o'clock on a Friday, it's time to focus on those you love. It's self-preservation. You have to have that cut-off point to sustain the job for the long term.

Rita Pierson
as told by her daughter Kristin Wright

Note from editor. When I decided to write a book about amazing, inspiring educators, I knew I had to include Rita Pierson. As a young teacher, I remember the Deputy Head playing her infamous Ted Talk video to us during a CPD session. It was a wet wintery evening and we were all exhausted. The last place we wanted to be was in that school hall listening to a lecture. But as soon as we heard Rita's opening words, in her inimitable style, we were captivated by her message. I knew right then that Rita Pierson was the kind of teacher I wanted to become. In the Ted Talk, Rita says that she once heard a colleague say: "They don't pay me to like the kids" and she responded, "Kids don't learn from people they don't like." She reaffirmed what I had already begun to realise, even at this early stage in my career, that teaching is all about relationships. She believed that every kid needs a champion – someone they can actually connect with on a real human, personal level. She believed that educators are born to make a difference and over her 40-year career, she certainly did. Speaking to her daughter Kristin and hearing about Rita from one of the people who knew her best was an amazing experience and it made me admire her even more. She may have sadly passed away but her legacy will live on in all the pupils she nurtured and championed in her incredible career.

My mother Rita was a native Houstonian, the only child to two educators; my grandfather taught History (ironically named Julius Cesar) and my grandmother taught 4th grade for forty years, all at the same elementary school. There is no doubt that this influenced her decision to be an educator. She taught special education and speech therapy - very inconvenient having a Mom who could read your lips! She was also an elementary school counsellor and afterwards, an assistant principal.

Her teaching career began right out of college, when she finished from Elmhurst College, right outside of Chicago. She went away to school in 1969, when integration was still evolving here, so going away to school, to a predominantly white institution, was a big deal. Unfortunately, I don't know the name of the school she taught at after graduating but it's the school she refers to in her famous TED Talk. Her first husband was a brilliant teacher (as she described him), perhaps this also influenced her early career. Both my mother and grandmother were master relationship builders. This led to my mum's ideology, which was focused on making connections and building and maintaining trust. These relationships were always built on mutual respect. She taught through storytelling, comedy and pure love and even when she didn't like a kid, she still loved them. It guided how she taught and her students always kept her going as a teacher, they were her driver. She is absolutely the model I followed myself as an educator; she always taught the kids no one else wanted to deal with and was often the end of the line for kids.

Of course, being a teacher is never without its challenges and these were usually centred around other adults: administrators who were detached from the classroom or parents who wanted to be rude. She once had a parent who couldn't (or wouldn't) get the child to school on time. The issue became so bad that truancy officers were about to get involved and take the parent to court. My Mom called a meeting with the parent and the parent's explanation was "we don't believe in alarm clocks for the kids. We allow them to get up whenever their body sees fit. We also allow them to fall asleep whenever their body feels tired." Her reply was "Thank you, that helps me understand a bit better. Perhaps when your child arrives to school, he should be allowed to wander the school until he chooses a classroom to enter. When he is hungry, he can go to the cafeteria and eat his fill. The child can then decide what bus he would like to ride home that day and even what house he might like to call home for the night." The parent was then ready to have a real conversation about structure and its potential usefulness!

In 1991, my Mom earned her doctorate degree and it was so hard for her. There were no online classes or email options to share materials. I remember the study groups around our dining room table with other aspiring teacher leaders. She worked all day at school and some days we would drive straight to campus (Texas Southern University) for her evening classes, where I passed out tests and did my homework in the back on the floor. She worked on her dissertation all night, every night. We had an old word processor, basically an upgraded typewriter and the stress of it was terrible. We were all there the day she defended her dissertation: my dad, my two brothers, my godmother, my grandmother...she was amazing, a real-life superhero. We had to call her Dr. Mama for months!

Like many teacher's kids, I went to the same school that my Mom taught at; this was definitely a double-sided coin! We had corporal punishment and all teachers and administrators had a paddle. If you got in trouble, you got physically punished. But if I got into trouble, I got paddled by the teacher, and the teacher could give an immediate report to my Mom and then I was whooped AGAIN when I got home (by my dad, spanking was never her style!) It happened ONCE, I was a quick learner! But the pros definitely outweighed the cons. Teachers stay late which means teacher's kids stay late too, so I was free to explore the halls, help put up bulletin boards, or enjoy snacks out of the forbidden teacher's lounge. Teacher's kids were like school royalty and riding to school together in the morning in our old raggedy Cadillac was our thing. Our time. Even though the air didn't work and neither did the heat!

I never really meant to be a teacher but the universe willed me there anyway! My mother got the first run of every tale from the classroom, whether it was funny, shocking, sad, etc. She was the first person I called when I got in my car to go home every day. She was my professional sounding board and offered her genuine support on some of the toughest days in the classroom. I called her once to tell her I had been assigned a group of kids (1st graders) who were so below "standard" that I wasn't sure I was up to the task. These kids could not distinguish between letters and numbers, they couldn't write their names and some of them didn't even answer to their legal names (they had been called by their nickname since birth). I called her in a panic after the first day, even though this was my second or third year teaching, so I wasn't a novice. Her response was: "So quit. Grab your purse and go home. They can find a new teacher quickly if they move fast." She was so matter of fact about it! I told her that was crazy, that I couldn't quit. Where would they find another teacher so soon? She said "You're right. Now stop panicking and GO TEACH." Her advice was as clear then as it is now. No one, not even her, was coming to save me. The kids were mine, wherever they were academically and they were my responsibility.

In 2012, after forty years in education, my Mom was asked to film a TED Talk. That was huge for her. It was a massive honour, especially because this was their first TED Talk to be televised. The full show included John Legend as the host and a panel of other speakers that included Bill Gates and Jeffrey Canada. She was nervous because they wanted a written speech but my Mom NEVER wrote out what she was going to talk about when she presented, she was a natural teacher and a natural speaker. She accommodated of course and the rest is history. Later, she couldn't believe how many views it received online, even in the short time between recording it and her untimely passing in 2013. We were all so proud of her. Everyone we knew was watching the night it aired on PBS. I couldn't believe that this amazing woman on TV was my Mom. It took almost two years after her passing for me to be able to watch it again without sobbing. It's still hard. Telling you this is hard.

My Mom was so easy to love. She was funny and patient and she held such high standards for her students (and for me). The trick was, she never left you out on a limb by yourself. She was always there to support and encourage. I guess the same things that made her a fantastic educator are what also made her a great Mom. She took the tools my grandmother used – meeting kids where they are, being supportive but also incredibly expectant of the best, and combined them with high energy, comedy, structure and high expectations, all sprinkled with a bit of the unknown to keep the kids on their toes! All of this was wrapped in human connection and relationships, as she knew how important that part was to getting kids to learn.

My Mom, Rita Pierson, was a great champion of kids and educators. She would want teachers to remember how much power they wield in the classroom - that they have a profound responsibility to send kids out into the world better than when they got them. Building relationships is not about loose boundaries or being a kid's friend, it's about sharing who you are and being open to learning who they are in return. She would want teachers to recall her saying "Kids don't learn from people they don't like" and then work daily to be kind, kinder than they have to be. Kids don't experience enough kindness. As she so famously said, "every kid needs a champion."

Afterword

We often hear that the children of today are the leaders of tomorrow and that they will shape the future. But in order to become the leaders of tomorrow, children need excellent teachers to help them develop. The stories told in this book prove that teachers possess the skills and humanity to make a positive impact, to encourage and lay the foundations for their students' progress. No doubt, with their excellent guidance, their pupils will become forces of great change in society. Their impact will reach far beyond the confines of the schools they teach in.

It is not simply through their teaching, but also through their humanity and personal qualities that they have been able to have such an impact. Through all of their life experiences, their interests and passions, those things which truly make somebody human, they have been able to open up their students' hearts and light a spark in their pupils.

As this book demonstrates, teaching is not just a job, it is a mission. Those of us who embark upon this journey aim to transform lives. Our ethics underpin everything we do. The educators in this book are guided by a moral purpose which drives them to do the job they love. Some stories we read told of their own childhoods and how their own difficulties drove them to want to improve outcomes for others, while others had former careers, where they developed skills that have been invaluable to their careers today. Their strength and determination have been inspirational to younger generations and no more so than during the Covid-19 pandemic, where they tirelessly worked in incredibly demanding and challenging situations to provide not just an education for students but also often fed them.

Humans in the Classroom has been a celebration of teachers and educators, demonstrating that they are an invaluable resource. The stories in this book can be an inspiration to us all. It is a chance to say thank you to that inspirational teacher who had a profound effect on us and to celebrate the amazing work that teachers do every day in shaping and inspiring young minds, across the world.

References

Conroy, P. (1982) *The Lords of Discipline*. Boston: Mifflin Harcourt.

Jersild, A. T. (1955) *When teachers face themselves*. (14 ed.) Columbia: Teachers College Press.

Mazlish, B. (2012) 'From the sentiment of humanity t the concept of humanity.' *Historically Speaking*, 13(3) pp. 30-33.

Rogers, C.R. (1969) *Freedom to Learn: A view of what education might become*. Ohio: C.E. Merill Publishing Company.

TES (2019) 'It is worth it - teachers made our lives, say public.' [online] Available at: https://www.tes.com/news/it-worth-it-teachers-made-our-lives-say-public [Accessed 26 Aug. 2019].

Zehm, S. J., Kottler, J. A. (1993) *On being a teacher: the human dimension*. California: Corwin Press.

Acknowledgements

Writing a book has been a lifelong ambition – all I needed was an idea and when I got one, I didn't really know where to start. Without the encouragement and expertise of Doctor Debra Kidd, this book would have been just another idea – so thanks Debra for your guidance and support, when I was really quite clueless! Thanks, is also due to my publishers, McNidder and Grace Publishing who have been gentle and patient, never putting pressure on me and being understanding of me fitting this book around my teaching, studying and family commitments.

To the amazing teachers who took time out of their busy schedules to speak to me, open their hearts and share their experiences with me...I thank you from the bottom of my heart. Your stories have enriched my life and I have learnt so much from your experiences.

Most importantly, to my family and mostly, my amazing husband Mike. Despite holding down your own important job in university education, you have taken over the reigns at home, often losing me or whole evenings and weekends while I was speaking on the telephone, transcribing interviews or feverishly typing away on edits. I love you and couldn't have done this without you. I owe any successes I get to you and I hope I can make you all proud.

Finally, to all of the children I have taught across my career – the difficult ones, the delightful ones, the ones who were finding their own way in the world, each of you have taught me something about myself and I hope I left you with some positive memories. I hope you saw me as a human being, not just your teacher. This book is for you.